DRAWING HEAVEN
into Your MARRIAGE

Powerful Principles with Eternal Results

H. Wallace Goddard, PhD

Meridian Publishing
10504 Sideburn Court
Fairfax, VA 22032-2600
USA

Order information: www.ldsmag.com/books.

Small portions of this work are drawn from earlier
works by the author.

All quotes used by permission of author,
Church Intellectual Properties, or Deseret Book

This publication is neither sponsored nor endorsed by
The Church of Jesus Christ of Latter-day Saints.

Printed in the United States of America
ISBN: 978-1-934537-02-2

ACKNOWLEDGMENTS

There are several people who have tirelessly read drafts of these chapters and offered wise counsel. Chief among them is Barbara Keil who has an extraordinary gift for seeing the big picture and capturing it with carefully crafted language. I am also grateful to Greg Clark, Kristin Allen, Geoff Steurer, Jim Brown, Justin Coulson, and Jim Ashman who have contributed insightful feedback and gentle encouragement. Special thanks to Darla Isackson who has patiently and capably edited this book.

Thanks to those who have taught me about this important subject—scholars and friends. Many people have trusted me with their fragile feelings and eternal hopes. I honor their seeking.

Thanks to you, kind reader, for your efforts to bring more kindness and goodness to the world we all share.

Thanks also to the children Nancy and I have been blessed with, their spouses, and their children for their patience with me as I learn to practice what I preach.

Thanks to my wonderful parents and ancestors who planted a love of life and family deep in my soul.

Thanks to Scot and Maurine Proctor who have labored to bless the world with truth through *Meridian Magazine*—and who have allowed me to be one of the voices on *Meridian*. They are changing the world with their tireless and visionary efforts.

Thanks to the most patient and kind person I have ever known, my dear wife, Nancy. She is simply the best Christian and friend I know. I love her dearly and am eternally grateful for her patience with me as I toil to have my performance catch up with my knowledge.

Most of all, thanks to a Perfect Father who developed a perfect plan. Thanks to His beloved Son who redeemed us all from hopeless loss by His perfect love and sacrifice. May all of Creation rejoice in the opportunity they have provided us!

DEDICATION

For my beloved Nancy

CONTENTS

INTRODUCTION

From Misery to Joy

Mom says I was a pleasant baby. As I grew, I must have become less pleasant. I remember spending a lot of my growing-up years annoying and battling my siblings. I suppose that struggles with siblings teach all of us many maladaptive lessons, as they did me.

We're probably not deliberately malicious. In fact our official theology tells us that children are born innocent (see D&C 93:39). But innocent isn't the same as charitable, and as we struggle to secure a place in the life and love of the family, we frequently develop some uncharitable and ungenerous characteristics.

When I attempted to inventory some of the maladaptive skills I developed in my youth, I came up with the following list. Consider whether you developed some of these attitudes and abilities in your childhood.

- Put my own needs first lest my needs go unmet. (Go for the biggest piece of cake.)
- Defend myself. (Don't show weakness. Return fire for fire.)
- See the other person as guilty. (Consider even innocent behavior as aggressive or selfish.)

- Zero in on weaknesses in others. (Notice what makes others crazy and be prepared to bombard them.)
- Make fun of and minimize the other person. (Treat others with disdain.)
- Color the truth. (Tell stories in ways that make me look innocent, my sibling guilty.)
- Argue their wickedness persuasively. (Describe their faults derisively.)
- Be aware of the audience. (Take advantage of Mom and Dad's irritations with the enemy sibling.)
- Hurt them and keep them afraid. (Learn the tools of terrorism.)

It's amazing what awful things we can learn in the course of growing up. I think these tendencies underscore the literal truth of the Lord's message to Adam: "Inasmuch as thy children are conceived in [a world of] sin, even so when they begin to grow up, sin conceiveth in their hearts" (Moses 6:55, emphasis added). This world teaches us to look after ourselves at all costs. Truly, the natural child—the one who attends only to his own needs—is an enemy to siblings (see Mosiah 3:19).

CARRYING THE LESSONS INTO MARRIAGE

As we grow up and enter adult relationships, consider how maladaptive such oft-practiced thoughts and behaviors can be. Consider each item on my list once more—this time in the context of marriage.

- Put my own needs first lest my needs go unmet. (Go for the biggest piece of cake.)
- Defend myself. (Don't show weakness. Return fire for fire.)
- See the other person as guilty. (Consider even innocent behavior as aggressive or selfish.)
- Zero in on weaknesses in others. (Notice what makes others crazy and be prepared to bombard them.)
- Make fun of and minimize the other person. (Treat others with disdain.)

- Color the truth. (Tell stories in ways that make me look innocent, my sibling guilty.)
- Argue their wickedness persuasively. (Describe their faults derisively.)
- Be aware of the audience. (Take advantage of Mom and Dad's irritations with the enemy sibling.)
- Hurt them and keep them afraid. (Learn the tools of terrorism.)

These lessons for childhood survival do not contribute to healthy marital functioning. Their awfulness is reminiscent of the mother who overheard her little girl and a neighbor child playing house. They decided to get married, and the little girl began the vows: "You have the right to remain silent. Anything you say can and will be used against you in a court of law. You may now kiss the bride." If we are to have a strong marriage, we must put off the natural man and learn better ways.

A painful and realistic portrayal of marriage was provided by a man who submitted this question to an online family service.

"After 13 years of marriage, I've come to realize that I really don't like my wife. She is everything that I despise in a wife and a person. I'm a religious man, have tried everything the books say, and have taken direct orders from our pastor to implement actions all in an effort to cause a positive change in the marriage. The bottom line is, I see no positive aspects to my wife's personality, and it taints all of her relationships, especially ours. I really dislike being around her and I've run out of solutions. Just short of divorce, is there anything that can be done as a final effort to salvage this marriage? BC in NM"

Is the major problem in this marriage the wife's shortcomings? Probably not. Later in this book I quote a colleague who says, "When people are upset and angry, they are blind to any position but their own."

CAN ANYTHING BE DONE?

The Lord has provided the cure for the childhood lessons we learned in self-defense. Perhaps He intended that we learn these higher lessons in our growing-up years—though most of us learn them imperfectly if at all.

"Therefore I give unto you a *commandment* [A commandment!], to *teach these things freely unto your children,* [Note what is to be taught!] saying: "That by reason of transgression cometh the fall, which *fall bringeth death,* and inasmuch as ye were born into the world by water, and blood, and the spirit, which I have made, and so became of dust a living soul, even so *ye must be born again into the kingdom of heaven,* of water, and of the Spirit, and be cleansed by blood, even the blood of mine Only Begotten; that ye might be sanctified from all sin, and enjoy the words of eternal life in this world, and eternal life in the world to come, even immortal glory" (Moses 6:58-59, emphasis added).

Without a new birth, we will never be what we should be in marriage. We will drag our sick, troubled, tortured ways into every encounter and every relationship. God invites us to bury the diseased natural man and be born again as new creatures in Christ.

But, can the gospel of Jesus Christ really help us function better in the day-to-day challenges of marriage?

SURPRISED BY THE DOCTRINE

On one occasion an earnest, intelligent, LDS mother sought me out for advice. "My husband is a good man, but I no longer find him attractive. I am thinking about leaving him. But I am not sure if it is right."

I really wanted to help this good woman find answers to her dilemma. I hoped my training in relationships and my years of marriage would help. I prayed for guidance.

Much to my surprise I found myself talking to her about the Atonement of Christ. All my training in family life protested: "What does that have to do with her dilemma?" But my spirit would not be deterred. An hour of testifying of His inestimable goodness, mercy, and love spilled out. Phrases from the great Atonement chapters in the Book of Mormon came to life. The cup of testimony was brim with joy.

After it all spilled out, I paused, wondering how to apply the doctrine of the Atonement to her dilemma. But her face told me that nothing more needed to be said. The Atonement of Jesus Christ was the answer. Because of His goodness, we are reconciled to God. When we are reconciled to God, we are reconciled to each other. His goodness makes us one.

Filled with charity—that sweet and divine gift of heavenly love—she felt a renewed bond with her husband. She chose to stay with him. Gladly. Joyously. Lovingly. Their marriage is strong today.

The answers are in the Principles

The Gospel of Jesus Christ—that great plan of happiness—provides the solutions for our humanness. Having suffered the bitter fruits of badness, it invites us to prize the good fruits of gospel-anchored relationships (see Moses 6:55).

Most marriage programs emphasize a set of skills to help partners express discontents in fair, non-attacking ways. The assumption is that every marriage has its discontents and that those must be processed in non-destructive ways in order for the relationship to function well.

My assumption is very different. I believe that the key to a healthy relationship is being a healthy, saintly, God-seeking person—to be born again—to be a new creature in Christ. When we are more godly, fewer things bother us. And when we run into problems, we are more likely to process them in helpful ways.

Notice that God offers just one single escape clause from our desperate mortal, fallen situation: "For the natural [spouse] is an enemy to God [and his or her partner], and has been from the fall of Adam, and will be, forever and ever, *unless* [Here comes the escape clause!] he *yields to the enticings of the Holy Spirit, and putteth off the natural man and becometh a saint through the atonement of Christ the Lord*" (Mosiah 3:19, emphasis added).

In the upcoming chapters, I will discuss the core gospel principles and describe the ways they can take us from our self-serving and self-centered traditions of the natural spouse—the spouse unchanged by the Spirit of God—toward the good and gracious ways of godliness. These are the First Principles of Eternal Marriage. These are the principles that will enable us to draw heaven into our marriages. These powerful principles can have eternal results.

CHAPTER ONE

THE PLAN:

"Marriage is ordained of God."

*"And again, verily I say unto you, that whoso forbiddeth
to marry is not ordained of God, for marriage is ordained
of God unto man." (D&C 49:15)*

The Lord is very clear in His attitude about marriage. Marriage is designed and endorsed by Him. Marriage is ordained of God. *Ordained.* To ordain means to authorize or order by virtue of superior authority. To ordain is stronger than approving of. It is closer to commanding. So marriage is ordained, endorsed, or commanded by God unto man.

But what is God's purpose for marriage? Did God design marriage as a refuge—a safe haven—from a troubled world? Or did He design marriage as a laboratory where each of us could conduct daily experiments in gospel living? Or did he design marriage as a spiritual challenge course to humble us, stretch us, and refine us?

Yes, to all of the above. For most people, marriage is sometimes a refuge from the storm. At other times marriage *is* the storm where cold squalls and pitching decks test our balance and determination as we seek the promised land of marital harmony.

One thing is sure. God did not design marriage as a retirement village where we sunbathe, work the buffet, and play golf. When God ordained marriage, He had loftier and more demanding purposes in mind.

When we understand God's purposes for marriage, we are more

likely to feel blessed by it. *And* we are less likely to feel disappointed and persecuted by it.

The keys to surviving and enjoying marriage are found in the Gospel of Jesus Christ.

Where do we find the solutions for marriage's stern challenges? What are the tools God would have us use? Since God's objective is to help us develop godly character, He has provided a set of tools perfectly designed to help us master the challenges of marriage (and life in general): the Gospel of Jesus Christ!

We will only succeed at marriage as we use eternal gospel principles to become more of what God has invited us to become. Marriage is God's graduate school for advanced training in Christian character. Those truly succeeding at marriage are those who are applying the Gospel of Jesus Christ in their lives.

"The Family: A Proclamation to the World" declares the enduring truth that happiness in family life is most likely to be achieved if founded on the teachings of our Lord and Savior.[1] We could go even a step farther. Perhaps enduring and soul-filling happiness in marriage is *only* found by actively using the principles of Jesus' gospel.

Douglas Brinley has suggested that, "our entire [LDS] theology is geared to help us succeed as married companions."[2] President Packer has confirmed the formula: "If you seek for a cure that ignores faith and religious doctrine, you look for a cure where it never will be found."[3]

The key to a satisfying marriage is to be found in living the principles of the Gospel of Jesus Christ. There is no other place to find the solution.

How does this work? How can gospel truths help us solve the knotty and persistent problems of living and loving with another person? How do we translate faith, hope and charity into sweet and productive companionship?

Brother Brinley suggests that understanding doctrine softens our hearts and leads to Christ-like behavior, which culminates in happy marriages.[4] Rather than learn a set of skills for dealing with difficulties, we seek a change of heart.

That is a tall order. I have worked for a lifetime to get a change of heart. There have been small successes and lots of failures.

What changes hearts? The following scripture gives the formula: "As many of them as are brought to the knowledge of the truth, and to know of the wicked and abominable traditions of their fathers, and are led to believe the holy scriptures, yea, the prophecies of the holy prophets, which are written, which leadeth them to faith on the Lord, and unto repentance, which faith and repentance bringeth a change of heart unto them" (Helaman 15:7).

Perhaps we have badly underestimated the power of the doctrine of Christ to transform our lives and relationships.

A STORY WITH TRANSFORMING POWER

Jesus spoke a parable that can change the way we think about all our relationships. This is a unique story, one of the greatest stories ever told by anyone anywhere. This amazing parable gives us a perfect metaphor for marriage and life: a journey. It was designed by the Perfect Teacher to enrich our understanding of His purposes. In the pages ahead consider the story and its interpretation. See if it holds precious surprises for you as it has for me.

The story was evoked from the Master by a devious and malevolent question. "And, behold, a certain lawyer stood up and tempted him saying, Master, what shall I do to inherit eternal life?" (Luke 10:25). A Jewish expert in the law set a trap for Jesus. He hoped to confound and disgrace Him.

As a side note, I must acknowledge that I have asked many questions of my dear wife with the same ungracious intent, such as: "Why in the world did you do that when you know we decided to do otherwise?" In asking such a question, I am not humbly seeking insight; I am seeking to humiliate my partner. I am acting like a lawyer looking for a conviction. That is not a good way to strengthen a relationship.

Perhaps I am not alone. Perhaps you also have cross-examined your partner with the intent to humiliate and shame her or him. For any who have asked or who have been asked a mean-spirited question, Jesus provided the model response.

RESPONDING WITH GRACE

Perfect Jesus set the perfect example. Running counter to the universal human tendency, He did not react to the dishonesty of the question. Nor did He try to outmaneuver the attacker. He did not even play to the weak side of the questioner. Notice how wisely and graciously Jesus crafts his reply: "What is written in the law? How readest thou?" (v. 26).

Jesus—sweet, exemplary Jesus—invited the lawyer to cite the law. He invited the lawyer to put his talents to noble (rather than ignoble) purpose. In effect He said, "I know that you are an expert in the law. Based on your study, what would your answer be?"

If my questions and replies were inspired by the same graciousness, would I be a better husband? Rather than bringing a spirit of accusation to our frustrations, we can bring a spirit of reconciliation and kindness. I might comment, "Your decision surprises me. Would you tell me about your thoughts in making that decision?" If we listen humbly and charitably, we will appreciate the logic behind our partner's decision. We might still favor a different option, but we can be gracious about his or her decision.

For any who have been asked a malicious, accusatory question, Jesus is still the model. If our partner attacks us with malicious questions, we, like Jesus, can respond with grace. If we follow Jesus' lead, we will neither use malicious questions nor respond to them in kind. Instead, we will invite our partner to join us in solving a problem.

After Jesus had asked about the law, the lawyer replied to Jesus' query with familiar words: "Thou shalt love the Lord thy God with all thy heart, and with all thy soul, and with all thy strength, and with all thy mind; and thy neighbour as thyself" (v.27).

I wish the scriptural account gave us more detail about the spirit in which the answer was given. Since the lawyer's questions before and after this answer were given with malevolent intent, we might assume that this rendering of the law was given in an impatient, condescending way. Perhaps he rolled his eyes and smirked as he answered the Master's question.

Yet Jesus acknowledged the answer: "Thou hast answered right: this do, and thou shalt live" (v.28). Jesus did not launch a follow-up lecture. He allowed the interest of the lawyer to drive the conversation, a wise course for us in families. Most of the lectures I have given to family members are not only unproductive, they are counterproductive. Most of my lecturing and cross-examining fits the description given in the following scripture:

"When we undertake to *cover our sins,* or to *gratify our pride,* our vain ambition, or to *exercise control* or dominion or compulsion upon the souls of the children of men, in any degree of unrighteousness, behold, the heavens withdraw themselves; the Spirit of the Lord is grieved; and when it is withdrawn, Amen to the priesthood or the authority of that man" (D&C 121:37, emphasis added).

When we insult the dignity of family members, we create a system of resentment and spite. We lose any influence we could have had. As Jesus ably demonstrated, a simple and gentle answer is best. Often less is more.

Goodness that sees beyond the present

"But [the lawyer], *willing to justify himself,* said unto Jesus, And who is my neighbour?" (v.29, emphasis added) Jesus clearly recognized the sneaky, nasty intent of the lawyer, but rather than confront and lecture him, He taught and invited him with a parable that challenges us all, a story that can teach us the central purposes of life. Maybe when we feel attacked by our partners, we might revisit the story told by the Master.

It is also worth considering what the reason was that Jesus treated such a relentlessly malicious lawyer with such graciousness. Why would Jesus return beauty for ashes? Did He know something about the lawyer that was not evident to anyone else? Or was He more focused on goodness and graciousness than anyone else?

I suspect that both are true. I think that Jesus honored the malicious lawyer with such grace because He knew that there was underdeveloped tenderness inside the man. Under layers of prejudice and small-mindedness, there was a seed of goodness waiting for life-bestowing water. Jesus is the Water that gives life.

I also believe that Jesus is remarkably focused on goodness. It is His nature "to give unto them beauty for ashes, the oil of joy for mourning, the garment of praise for the spirit of heaviness; that they might be called trees of righteousness, the planting of the LORD, that he might be glorified" (Isaiah 61:3). Jesus is the model of charity.

What a glorious example for any of us who ever dealt with disappointment with another person! As we follow His example, we look for goodness even where none may be evident. We become "relentless in our redemptiveness," as Elder Maxwell said of Jesus.[5]

So Jesus offers the hard man an amazing parable, a redemptive story:

THE JOURNEY OF LIFE

"A certain man went down from Jerusalem to Jericho . . ." (v. 30). Notice that, in this account, we have no identifying information about the central character of the story. Was he a merchant, a foreigner, a father, an apostate? Why are we given no detail about that poor man who made the lonely trek to Jericho? Because that traveler represents you and me and our partners and our children in our journeys of life. He is every man and every woman and every child. Jesus is telling a story about us, about you and me.

There is unexpected significance that the journey was from Jerusalem to Jericho. Jerusalem had unique spiritual significance. It was the Holy City. It was the temple city. Its elevation would not normally be noteworthy—except in contrast to that of Jericho. "From *Jerusalem, at 2,700 feet above sea level, to Jericho, at 850 feet below sea level the lowest city on the globe,* is a descent of over 3,500 feet."[6] Jesus' choice of those particular endpoints for the journey must have significance. Were the two cities chosen specifically because Jesus was teaching of everyman's descent from the heavenly presence to this hellish world? Was Jesus inviting us to understand this parable as a type for each of our mortal journeys? We might paraphrase the story: "Each of us goes down from the presence of God to this lowly, desolate world." Jesus is talking about our own inglorious descents from Heaven.

". . . and fell among thieves" (v. 30).

The risks of a lone journey along the road to Jericho were well known to the Jews of the time. Why did the traveler take the risks? And why do we take the risks of mortality? Why did we choose to come to this desolate place?

A HEAVENLY ONE-ON-ONE

In my mind I picture a time ages ago when Father called you and me— each of us individually—to a Father's Interview. He looked on us with love and shared His appreciation for us: "I love you, Dear One."

Then He told us: "You are ready to go to earth." We tensed at the prospect of leaving Him. He continued: "I can customize your earth experience to prepare you for the place you want in Eternity. So the key question is, where do you want to spend Eternity?"

Each of us trembled. Dared we say? Dared we hope? He prodded: "Go ahead. Tell me. Please."

We blurted: "Oh Father! I want to be with you! I want to be a part of your work! I want to spend Eternity with Jehovah and all the noble and great ones." Then we hung our heads in shame. How dare we hope for such a thing? How could we be so presumptuous?

But He gently lifted our chins. I imagine a tear coursing down His face. "And that is where *I want you*. I want you back with Me and all my most cherished ones." He pulled each of us close and filled our spirits with His goodness. We leaned into His love and felt more at home than we ever had. After what seemed like an eternity, He leaned back and sighed. "The education for exaltation is very rigorous and demanding . . ."

We interrupted: "Oh! I'd do anything to be with You again." He smiled, but had a concerned look in His eyes. "Let me show you something." He opened our minds to see every hour, every minute, every second, every hiccough of our personal mortal experience. After all, He is not a person to sneak big surprises into the small print of our mortal contracts. In my opinion, He showed us every single thing we would experience in our mortal education from the pains of birth to the anxieties of death and every struggle in between. We were sobered.

He asked, "Would you bear all of that to return Home?"

"Gladly. But . . ." We hesitated. "Can I do it? Am I strong enough? Am I good enough? Do I have a chance of making it?"

Father replied. "No, you can't make it on your own. You would get hopelessly lost. You will often be confused and uncertain. You will become forlorn and dispirited. But, if you're willing to go, I'll provide my two Extraordinary Helpers. I will provide you my Third-in-command, the Holy Spirit, who will teach you, comfort you, and cleanse you. And I will provide my Second-in-command, my dearly Beloved Son, who will give you the teachings you need. And He will pay the price of all your debts so that you can come Home clean and perfect." Father glowed.

At this point our eyes were big with amazement and tears coursed down our cheeks. We slipped from His arms to our knees "You would do all that for me?"

"Gladly."

"And all the morning stars sang together, and all the sons of God shouted for joy" (Job 38:7). Never in all of eternity had there been such Good News! Right then and there we committed to make the perilous journey. We signed the contract. We made a covenant.

However, somewhere between our Heavenly Home above to the bedeviled and beleaguered earth beneath, we suffered from a veil that hid that sacred pre-trip moment from our view. So we started this journey dazed, forgetful, and vulnerable. As newborn babies we cry and flail our limbs. This cold and breezy place is clearly not our Home. The bad news is that things will get worse before they get better. Our mortal pathways are strewn with thorns and thistles (see Moses 4). As we journey through mortality in this harsh world, we continue to be vulnerable to brutal attacks. We often fall among thieves.

THE TREACHEROUS JOURNEY

". . . and fell among thieves, which stripped him of his raiment, and wounded him, and departed, leaving him half dead" (v. 30).

What a perfect description of what every person experiences in the course of mortality! We all get injured and left alone along our treacherous journey of life. We lose the robe of innocence and heavenly grace.[7] We are often stripped of our hope and whatever dim sense of identity we had. We are wounded not only by difficulties but also by sin and filth. We are left exactly half dead. While our bodies still breathe, our spirits are dead—cut off from the Divine Lifeblood that sustained us when we walked in the Garden of Heaven with Father.

Each of us is wounded in mortality. No one is spared. Ironically, those who have the highest aspirations suffer some of the hardest injuries. They chose the tougher training.

However, if we learn the mindset of faith, our troubles no longer surprise us nor bother us so much. We know that everything we suffer was carefully designed by a Perfect Father to prepare us for our Work on High. We also know that the entire First Presidency of Heaven is looking after us.

HOPING FOR HELP

"And by chance there came down a certain priest that way . . ." (v. 31)

Ahhh! We are hopeful! Priests are those people in the community commissioned to see to the well-being of the people. They are the spiritually elite. Certainly this priest will stop and care for our injuries.

". . . and when he saw him, he passed by on the other side." (v. 31)

Yikes! Why would he do such a thing? He did not merely pass by, he went out of his way to avoid the disagreeable sight. What was he thinking? Maybe: "What a shame that people would be out on this dangerous road alone. Doesn't he know any better? What a fool! This is the natural consequence of such a foolish decision. I hope he learns a lesson. Besides, he is not in my congregation." There is a cool detachment, maybe even some condescension in such a response.

Here comes the next passerby. Certainly he will stop. After all, he is a Levite, one who serves as a musician or custodian in the temple of God. Such a humble servant will certainly minister to one who is injured.

"And likewise a Levite, when he was at the place, came and looked on him and passed by on the other side" (v.32).

Was convenience or cleanliness more important to the Levite than godly compassion? What a bitter irony! Was Jesus suggesting that the entire Jewish hierarchy from humble Levites to exalted priests was spiritually bankrupt? Was He saying that charity is the mark of true followers—and there was none of it in the ancient and rigid order?

Certainly the same might be said of some of our responses to spousal suffering in marriage. We sometimes are so concerned about being right in an argument that we fail to be good. When the system is drained of charity, it is only a dead form. "The letter killeth but the spirit giveth life" (2 Corinthians. 3:6). When we pound our spouse with logic or power, we are no better than the thieves. When we dispassionately witness our partners' pains, we are no better than the priest or Levite.

We can be humbled by reflection. How often have I seen my partner's pain and added to it by heaping discontent on my already-injured spouse? When she is hurting do I take an "I told you so" stance?

Maybe we do a little better than the thieves. Maybe we act like the priest or Levite. We blithely ignore our partner's struggles. Maybe we figure they deserve it. Maybe we figure it's not our problem. Maybe we are absorbed with our own problems.

If still conscious, after the priest and Levite passed by, the injured one must have been desperate. The holiest members of his community had passed him by. Would no one have pity on one as miserable and helpless as he? It would appear that he had no hope as he weakened at the side of the road.

UNEXPECTED GRACE

"But a certain Samaritan, as he journeyed, came where he was . . ." (v. 33).

Certainly he will not get help from a Samaritan. They are half-breed pretenders to the great religious tradition. They are the lowest of the low. They are strangers and foreigners.

"The Samaritan was racially impure—half Gentile, half Israelite; he worshiped at a different temple, a rival of the Jerusalem temple. His religion was half pagan, half Jewish, *a blasphemous mongrel religion to the ultraorthodox Pharisees.* So Jews despised such people. . . . One can imagine how offensive this story was to the priests and Levites of Jesus' day. Translating such a parable into our culture, it is *as if a stake president or a bishop passed by such a victim because he was late for a session at the temple or a ward planning meeting, and an excommunicated Mormon cared for him.*"[8]

Note that the despicable Samaritan "journeyed" while the priest and likewise the Levite came "by chance." Is it possible that the officially religious came upon the scene by chance while the Samaritan was out looking for opportunities to serve? Is it possible that the most spiritual are not always those who appear most "religious"? Is it possible that the mark of a true believer is the willingness to travel the highways of life looking for opportunities to help those in need? Joseph Smith seemed to validate that idea when he said: "Love is one of the chief characteristics of Deity, and ought to be manifested by those who aspire to be the sons of God. A man filled with the love of God, is not content with blessing his family alone, but ranges through the whole world, anxious to bless the whole human race."[9]

There is a quirk in human nature here. Many of us find it easier to minister to the stranger than to the family member. Unexpected service to the stranger is often warmly appreciated. Service to family is expected and often goes unappreciated. As a result, many of us cheerfully do for others the things that we grudgingly or sporadically do for family. What would we do if we were less concerned about the rewards of appreciation? Probably we would offer gentle healing regularly to injured family members.

THE PATTERN OF HEAVENLY RESCUE

The Samaritan in Jesus' story clearly represents the Savior Himself. "Samaritans were viewed as the least of all humanity, so it was prophesied that the Servant Messiah would be 'despised and rejected of men' and 'esteemed . . . not'" (Isa.53:3).[10] The work of caring for the injured is often disdained by those who see themselves as holy or busy. Jesus is different:

". . . and when he saw him, he had compassion on him" (v. 33).

The first response of this disreputable stranger was compassion. Rather than chide the traveler for foolishness or lack of preparation, He looked on his injuries with empathy. Even now He does the same for us as He finds us bleeding by the side of the road. He might rightly claim that we have brought our miseries on ourselves. He might justly claim that He has no responsibility for us since we have all strayed from His counsel. But he looks on us with the compassion characteristic of God. We would not expect this Samaritan passerby to do more than feel saddened by our plight. Why would He care for those who cause Him pain? Yet again we are surprised by Him: The Samaritan "went to him, and bound up his wounds, pouring in oil and wine, and set him on his own beast, and brought him to an inn, and took care of him" (v.34).

Wow. The Stranger will bring all of His resources to bear in healing us, the injured ones! He binds up our wounds. He is, after all, One who is touched by every pain and infirmity that we ever suffer. He bore not only our sins but even our pains and discomforts so that His compassion would be fully informed (see Alma 7:11-12). He brings His whole soul as an offering to us.

SYMBOLS OF SPIRITUAL RESCUE

Hugh Nibley teaches us that no ancient Christian could have misunderstood the ceremonial implications of "pouring in oil and wine." The alert reader recognizes sacred, even sacramental, emblems. Today, when we think of oil, we recall hands laid on heads for healing. We think of anointing and dedicating our whole lives to sacred purposes. We are soothed and comforted by the blessings attended by consecrated oil.

J. A. Tvedtnes said, "olive oil is symbolic of the Holy Ghost. This is because the Holy Ghost provides spiritual nourishment, enlightenment, and comfort, just as olive oil in the ancient Near East was used for food, light, and anointing."[11]

When we think of the wine, we remember His weekly invitation to come boldly to the throne of grace and receive mercy and grace to help in time of need (Hebrews 4:16). Every week He offers His blood to heal us. With his stripes we are healed. His compassion stretches to the infinities of time and space as He personally ministers to all of us.

But there is still more. Jesus puts us on His beast and walks while we ride. What a model of meekness and humility! He, King of kings and Lord of lords, walks so that we may be carried to healing. He who is truly First becomes last while we who are last are put first.

Jesus does not then dump us at the first county hospital. He brings us to a safe place and tends to our healing Himself. In the time of our crisis, He stays up all night with us.

Perhaps you have felt His ministering to you in times of desperation. I have. And I am grateful. In our lonely nights He ministers to those of us who have slept through His agony (see Matthew 26:49).

CONTINUED CARE

"And on the morrow when he departed, he took out two pence, and gave them to the host, and said unto him, Take care of him; and whatsoever thou spendest more, when I come again, I will repay thee" (v. 35). After getting us through the crisis, he paid two pence to the host. The two pence can have several meanings. It could have provided care for the injured man for up to two months![12] How gracious that Jesus would provide such time for healing!

Or the two pence could have paid two days' wages for a laborer—

which could be understood as sustaining us in our labors while He is gone away after the crucifixion before returning on the third day with the resurrection.

There is a third interpretation to the two pence. Intriguingly, the amount paid was "the amount each Jewish man had to pay as the temple tax each year."[13] Thus this payment could be symbolic of putting the injured traveler right with God for a year while his body healed just as partaking of the sacrament worthily sets us right with God for another week of spiritual recovery.

THE REWARD FOR SERVICE

The account reports that Jesus leaves us in the care of the host with the promise to repay any expenses the man incurs above the amount already paid. Some commentators have noted the folly of anyone promising to pay any and all debts. It seems clear that Jesus is not turning the healing of the injured over to strangers. He is entrusting the work of ministering to those whom He knows and trusts, those who have made covenants with Him. He promises you and me that, when He comes again, He will repay anything we invest in helping and healing His children.

When we follow the example of the Good Samaritan and care for injured travelers, the currency of repayment for our service is uniquely appropriate if surprising. He promises us forgiveness of our sins. "For the sake of retaining a remission of your sins from day to day, that ye may walk guiltless before God—I would that ye should impart of your substance to the poor, every man according to that which he hath, such as feeding the hungry, clothing the naked, visiting the sick and administering to their relief, both spiritually and temporally, according to their wants" (Mosiah 4:26). When we minister to family members who are sick or injured, we receive in payment a divine bounty of forgiveness.

THE LOWEST RESPONSE TO VULNERABILITY

We see different kinds of responses to the traveler. The thieves seized on the opportunity to rob the traveler. The priest and Levite actively ignored him. The Samaritan had compassion and ministered to him. These three responses might represent general types of responses to those who are distressed.

When we operate by the telestial law, we act primarily to meet our own needs with disregard for others—just as the thieves did. Our automatic responses in family life usually operate at this level. Our needs are the guiding principle in our decisions. We act to protect our dignity and interests with little regard for the needs of family members.

For example, in a spousal squabble we attack our partners, their wisdom and goodness, in the process of proving that things should have been done our way. We leave them injured and half dead as we stomp off to inventory our rightness.

THE HONORABLE RESPONSE TO DISTRESS

The second type of response is the terrestrial typified by the priest and Levite and is guided by principles of fairness and honor. The priest and Levite had no official responsibility to one who was unwise or careless. Besides, how could they ever hope to help one who was so injured?

This level of functioning is actually about as good as humans can reasonably expect in family life. This is the mindset of honorable business. We give with the expectation of reasonable benefit. We negotiate and bargain. It is a triumph of the law of business over the law of the jungle.

When we don't get benefits commensurate with our investments, we cut our losses and quit the relationship. We have no intention of throwing good effort into hopeless causes.

THE HEAVENLY RESPONSE TO OUR NEED

The third type of response is that of the Samaritan. He was purposefully looking for those in need—such need is never in short supply in our families. And He came prepared. It was not by chance that He had oil, wine and bandages with Him. He was moved by compassion and prepared to serve.

This kind of response does not come easily to humans. In fact, I think it is fully impossible for us—unless we are filled with Jesus. We cannot "love [our] enemies, bless them that curse [us], do good to them that hate [us], and pray for them which despitefully use [us], and persecute [us]" (Matt. 5:44) unless we have been changed by Him.

Most of the time we exact an eye for an eye and a tooth for a tooth. Yet you can probably think of a time when you have responded to ugliness with graciousness, kindness, love, and compassion. It feels good. We can see Him working through us! We are blessed to have Him at the helm of our lives.

The surest test of our spiritual maturity is the way we react to those who are imperfect physically, spiritually, or emotionally. How do we react when someone attacks and blames us? Do we defend ourselves at all costs? Do we try to be fair and balanced? Or do we, like Jesus, recognize that ugliness is often an expression of pain? Do we minister with love and patience? Do we bring healing to the injured?

The change of heart

I used to assume that development was linear, that in our mortal journey we progress from our natural man telestial qualities toward fairness and a terrestrial state. Then we add an appreciation of Jesus and move to the celestial level. I was wrong.

There is no ladder we can climb from terrestrial thinking and acting to celestial thinking and acting. We do not become celestial by adding a pinch of Jesus to a terrestrial life. At some point we simply throw ourselves on His merits, mercy and grace. At some point we recognize that we may be able to keep ourselves from being the vilest of sinners, but if we are to be perfected, we must have His miraculous help (D&C 76:69; Mosiah 3:19).

The natural man must die and be born again as a spiritual being. That is the miracle. We do not climb out. He snatches us and delivers us to a new life. We make ourselves humble, and He makes us holy: "He that exalteth himself shall be abased; and he that humbleth himself shall be exalted" (Luke 18:14)! In the chapters ahead, I will talk about the gospel principles that change our hearts.

THE AFTERMATH OF THE PARABLE

We have not finished the great drama between Jesus and the lawyer. After blessing the lawyer with the remarkable story of the model Samaritan, Jesus invited him to identify the neighborly one: "Which now of these three, thinkest thou, was neighbour unto him that fell among the thieves? And he said, He that shewed mercy on him" (vv.36-7).

"He that showed mercy"!

How vital mercy is in family life! We forgive our parents of their flaws and limited knowledge. We forgive our partners for being human. We forgive our children for being children. Grace and mercy are at the heart of loving family life.

Then said Jesus unto him, "Go, and do thou likewise" (v.37). If we modeled our behavior after that of the Samaritan, our families would be heavenly.

The biblical account tells us nothing about the lawyer after his encounter with perfect Goodness and Grace. I look forward to the next life where I can learn the rest of the story. My hope is that the lawyer left that encounter humbled. He realized that his smallness had been met with largeness, his malice had been conquered by grace. I hope days of reflection and prayer led him to become a believer and a follower.

Who knows? Maybe he later became bishop of the Jerusalem 2nd Ward. Maybe he became a disciple who traveled the road of life looking for the injured so they could be healed with the balm of Jesus.

FUNDAMENTAL ATTRIBUTION ERROR

Social psychology has found an intriguing quirk in human thinking. The fundamental attribution error suggests that humans tend to interpret the behavior of others based on character—or lack of it. In contrast, when we interpret our own behavior, we tend to factor in circumstances as important.

For example, at the end of the day, I may believe that my partner accomplished so little because she is lazy or disorganized; I accomplished little because so many people made unexpected or unreasonable demands of me.

This bias is understandable. We usually know more about our own circumstances than about the circumstances of others. Yet you can see the mischief caused by this natural human programming. We tend to excuse our own failures while condemning others for theirs.

Because we know so little about the situations—and hearts—of others, we should be humble and cautious. We should not judge, except in the light of His perfect knowledge and love. "And now, my brethren, seeing that ye know the light by which ye may judge, which light is the light of Christ, see that ye do not judge wrongfully; for with that same judgment which ye judge ye shall also be judged" (Moroni 7:18).

THE GREAT HEALER

Jesus' infinite grace and goodness can conquer our smallness, selfishness, and peevishness. There is no arena of life where this conquest is more needed than in the scuffing and irritations of marriage. Marriage is perfectly designed to provoke us to desperation. It will sometimes leave us injured and half-dead. Priests and Levites—or therapists and advisors—will not ultimately rescue us. They may give us helpful pointers, but they cannot change our souls.

Success in marriage is much like the healing at Bethesda (see John 5:1-15). An invalid waited by the side of the pool with hopes of being healed by the magical waters. But it was Jesus who healed him. It was not the waters of the pool but the Water of Life that cured him. Many of us sit by the pool of the world's wisdom hoping to have our marriages healed. But it is Jesus—only Him and His truths—that transforms our marriages from crippled relationships to walking, working, dancing partnerships.

Just as the man who was healed at the pool of Bethesda did not initially know the identity of his benefactor, so many who succeed in marriage may not realize that the principles that bless their marriages are from Jesus. They may be following the light of Christ within them without knowing the Source. Still, He and His principles are the key.

He comes humbly to our broken-down hopes and offers to carry us to spiritual healing. Some of us resist. "No, thanks. I am waiting for an M.D. or other appropriate professional." We may not realize that all our problems are ultimately spiritual—and that Jesus is the great Healer. He heals every malady: "The Spirit of the Lord is upon me, because he hath anointed me to preach the gospel to the poor; he hath sent me to heal the brokenhearted, to preach deliverance to the captives, and recovering of sight to the blind, to set at liberty them that are bruised (Luke 4:18).

Regardless of our woe—whether irritation with spouse or trouble with anger—He is the One who can heal us.

THE CHALLENGE: CLIMBING OUT OF OUR MORTAL WEAKNESS

So, how do we, who are so woefully human, get from being thieves to being saviors on Mount Zion? The solution may begin in our minds. When we feel indignant or irritated, rather than take the feeling as some sure measure of truth, we can recognize the Lie—the idea that our instincts are right. Maybe they are the jangling of our self-preservation instincts. This is not the noblest part of us. So we learn to change the question. Instead of asking our partners questions such as:

- Why are you doing this to me?
- What's wrong with you?
- Don't you understand why this is important to me?
  We switch mindsets. We ask ourselves questions such as:
- I wonder if I can understand why this is important to my partner?
- What is my partner really telling me?
- I wonder if I can understand her pain?
- Can I get God to help me get beyond myself in order to understand my spouse?
- How would the Good Samaritan minister to my partner?

The surge of indignation that swells up when we are upset does not have to swamp our little boat. We can choose to calm the seas by the same power that Jesus used to calm the waters of Gennesaret. President McKay expresses well how we can use His goodness and power to calm storms of sea and soul: "The greatest need of this old world today is peace. The turbulent storms of hate, of enmity, of distrust, and of sin are threatening to wreck humanity. It is time for men—true men—to dedicate their lives to God, and to cry with the spirit and power of the Christ, 'Peace, be still' (Mark 4:39)." [14]

Yet ahead

This chapter is only a beginning. Our journey ahead includes chapters on other vital mindsets such as humility, faith, and charity. The powerful and surprising lessons Jesus can teach us on these subjects can prepare us to be better partners in the journey of marriage.

Along the way, I invite you to respond to the questions and suggestions at the end of each chapter. I call this exercise "Creating Your Own Story," since each of us has the opportunity of designing our own thoughts, feelings, and actions. Test these ideas and activities in the laboratory of your family life.

Creating Your Own Story

Sometimes we imagine that learning some tidy set of skills will enable us to process our partnership woes effectively. But good marriage is not about skills. It is about character. Consider the thoughts, feelings, and actions that are the measure of your character—and the key factors in a godly relationship.

Thoughts

What are some ways that your spouse is perfectly designed to help you grow spiritually?

How can you more gladly welcome the challenges that your spouse offers you?

Feelings

When we focus on our discontent, we are likely to blame any who have contributed to it. In contrast, when we focus on someone else's pains, we are more likely to have compassion. Do you feel compassion for your partner's difficulties and disappointments? Could you study what your partner's pains mean to him or her in order to cultivate your compassion?

Actions

When you see your partner in distress, do you go to him or her willing to offer help? Their distress may be as routine as feeling overwhelmed by the demands of an unusually busy day or as big as the death of a loved one. On occasions both small and large, do you stand ready to offer compassion and a helping hand?

What can you do to be better prepared to offer help in times of need?

NOTES

1   *Ensign*, November 1995, 102.

2   Douglas E. Brinley and D. K. Judd (Eds.), *Living in a Covenant Marriage*, Salt Lake City: Deseret Book [2004], 7.

3   "Families and Fences," *Improvement Era*, Dec. 1970, 106-07.

4   *Covenant Marriage*, 33.

5   Neal A. Maxwell, "'Jesus of Nazareth, Savior and King'," *Ensign*, May 1976, 26.

6   D. Kelly Ogden, "The Testing Ground for the Covenant People," *Ensign*, Sept. 1980, 56, emphasis added.

7   See J.W. Welch, "The Good Samaritan: A Type and Shadow of the Plan of Salvation," *BYU Studies*, 38 (2) [1999], 76.

8   T. M. Compton, "The Spirituality of the Outcast in the Book of Mormon," *Journal of Book of Mormon Studies*, Provo, UT: Foundation for Ancient Research and Mormon Studies, [1993], 2:153, emphasis added.

9 *Teachings of the Prophet Joseph Smith,* Compiled by Joseph Fielding Smith, Salt Lake City: Deseret Book, 1972, 174, emphasis added.

10 *Good Samaritan,* 79.

11 S. D. Ricks & J. W. Welch (Eds.), *The Allegory of the Olive Tree,* Salt Lake City: Deseret Book [1994], 427.

12 NIV Study Bible, New International Version published by Zondervan Bible Publishers in Grand Rapids, Michigan, 1560

13 *Good Samaritan,* 8

14 David O. McKay, *Gospel Ideals,* Salt Lake City, *Improvement Era,* 295.

Chapter Two

Obedience and Sacrifice:

"Willing to submit in all things"

Afflictions are the process by which God cultivates growth. Rather than dread our difficulties, we can learn to welcome them. We can learn to see them as blessings from heaven.

Since marriage is God's finishing school, we should expect more afflictions or challenges in marriage than in any other arena of life. I think of challenges among couples we know:

- She doesn't trust his judgment so she undermines all his decisions. He feels powerless and carps endlessly.

- He uses calm reasoning to organize his life—and judge his wife. She reacts emotionally and defensively to the judgments.

- She likes things organized. He takes a devil-may-care attitude. Both are chronically irritated with each other.

- He wants to make his wife happy. She has impossible dreams. He is endlessly in a frenzy trying to meet her needs.

- She is task-oriented—always working on a perfect home. He wants unlimited attention and admiration.

- He is gentle and deliberate. She races to decisions without giving him time to participate.

Regardless of whom we marry, there will inevitably be irritations. For example, one common difference is the acceptable level of tidiness and cleanliness. One person might feel that everything must be wrapped, sealed and protected from the pollution, chemicals, and carcinogens that are ever-present in the world. She worries about the microorganisms that conspire to spread ghastly diseases. She is likely to be married to a guy who will drop his peanut butter sandwich face down on the filthy garage floor and will gladly scrape it up and eat it. He might remove large contaminants—like cockroaches and hubcaps, but anything smaller than that he doesn't worry about. She will not eat anything that has been out of the fridge for more than 15 minutes. He would cook up road kill. The opportunity for irritation and judgment is vast! He may see her as neurotic. She may see him as irresponsible and foolish. How do any of us survive each other?

THE ESSENTIAL TENSION

In every relationship there is an inevitable tension. It is often worse in marriage than other relationships, in part because we share so much—money, time, food, space—even our own bodies. Marriage is not only intense but also can last for decades. As we are challenged to form our own little Zion, the natural man resists. "For the natural [spouse] is an enemy to God [and partner], and has been from the fall of Adam, and will be, forever and ever . . ." (Mosiah 3:19).

Our untamed, uncivilized, unconquered, unchanged natures are ill-suited for Zion. We have limited choices: to chafe and struggle in unsatisfying relationships, or put our natures on the altar for God to change, *or* we can depart Zion disenchanted. Those are the options. Man remains forever enemies to God and marriage—unless we yield "to the enticings of the Holy Spirit, and putteth off the natural man and becometh a saint through the atonement of Christ the Lord, and becometh as a child, submissive, meek, humble, patient, full of love, willing to submit to all things which the Lord seeth fit to inflict upon him, even as a child doth submit to his father" (Mosiah 3:19).

This choice and change is not a once-and-for-all decision. Most of us are quite determined to love perfectly when we make covenants to each other. But we put off the natural man if the resolve is to last. Even if we have had a mighty change of heart—even if at some time in our lives God has filled our souls—every day we decide anew whether to live by the guidelines of the mind of Christ or the imperatives of the natural man. Every day, every hour we decide whether we will continue to sing the song of redeeming love—or whimper in discontent.

With practice, the choice to sing the song of redeeming love will become easier and more automatic. Yet every day we must choose: "Wherefore, men are free according to the flesh; and all things are given them which are expedient unto man. And they are free to choose liberty and eternal life, through the great Mediator of all men, or to choose captivity and death, according to the captivity and power of the devil; for he seeketh that all men might be miserable like unto himself" (Nephi 2:27).

LEARNING FROM THIS EARTH'S FIRST COUPLE

Adam and Eve are the models or archetypes for our life experience. Where they have led, we follow. What they have done, we are expected to do. So we study their lives for direction.

Adam and Eve had every reason to be gloomy about life in this world. They had lived in serene and peaceful abundance. Then they were evicted and sent to the slums. Eve's sorrow was multiplied and the ground was cursed for Adam's sake.

Was this a tragedy? No. It was a brave step toward eternal accomplishment. Note the encouraging truth nested in the words of the curse: "Cursed shall be the ground *for thy sake;* in sorrow shalt thou eat of it all the days of thy life" (Moses 4:23, emphasis added).

The curse was and is a blessing. Through our labors and struggles, we will learn to know good from evil. We will suffer the bitter taste of evil. We will learn to enjoy the sweet fruits of goodness. We can learn to choose and cherish the good.

FOLLOWING THEIR EXAMPLE

Imagine the terrible loneliness and emptiness that assaulted Adam and Eve as they left their garden home for an unknown and hostile world where thorn, thistle, and noxious weeds tormented them.

We have all felt as Adam and Eve felt. At times we miss our idyllic Home terribly. We long to be there. But we are shut out. The yearning creates a continuing pang of loneliness. Even in their loneliness, Adam and Eve were an example to us. "And Adam and Eve, his wife, called upon the name of the Lord" (Moses 5:4).

THE ONLY AND SURE REMEDY

The only remedy for our loneliness is to call upon God. When we feel hopeless, lost, and desperate, we should call upon Father. In return we, like Adam and Eve, will be shown the path for our journey Home. "And [God] gave unto them commandments, that they should worship the Lord their God, and should offer the firstlings of their flocks, for an offering unto the Lord. And Adam was obedient unto the commandments of the Lord" (Moses 5:5).

Adam and Eve were to offer God their very best, the "firstlings of their flocks." I wonder what the firstlings of our flocks are. Is it our cherished free time that we must put on the altar? Is it our love for sports, games, reading, shopping, clothes, or money that must be sacrificed?

PAYING HEAVEN'S PRICE

Most of us want the prize without paying the price. We want to have a close, loving marriage, but we're not willing to give up our pet affections. But God has required us to make sacrifices if we are to enjoy that which is most valuable. John Taylor quoted Joseph Smith as making this statement about sacrifice:

> You will have all kinds of trials to pass through. And it is quite as necessary for you to be tried as it was for Abraham and other men of God, and God will feel after you, and He will take hold of you

and wrench your very heart strings, and if you cannot stand it you will not be fit for an inheritance in the Celestial Kingdom of God.[15]

We cannot steal the fire of love from heaven. We must buy it with soul-stretching payments.

DAILY INSTALLMENTS ON HEAVENLY GOODS

In the continuing story of Adam and Eve, God has given us further directions for our growth in marriage. "And after many days an angel of the Lord appeared unto Adam, saying: Why dost thou offer sacrifices unto the Lord? And Adam said unto him: I know not, save the Lord commanded me" (Moses 5:6).

It is clear that Adam and Eve were obedient. Even as they daily faced privation and desperation, they continued to worship God and make sacrifices. They continued to trust God's counsel. Faith is fundamental, just as H. E. Fosdick observed: "We must believe that there is a purpose running through the stern, forbidding process. What men have needed most of all in suffering, is not to know the explanation, but *to know that there is an explanation.* And religious faith alone gives confidence that human tragedy is *not* the meaningless sport of physical forces, making our life what Voltaire called it, 'a bad joke.'"[16]

Faith is the stubborn resolve to see God blessing us in all circumstances. Even in our struggles and disappointments, faith requires us to believe God is ministering to us.

BEING LED ALONG THE PATH

In return for their obedience, their trust in God, Adam and Eve were taught from On High. "And then the angel spake, saying: This thing is a similitude of the sacrifice of the Only Begotten of the Father, which is full of grace and truth" (Moses 5:7).

Wow! So much truth in one verse! When we make sacrifices, we are following the example of the Savior, who sacrificed everything in order to rescue us. The making of holy sacrifices is full of grace and truth.

The willingness to put our preferences on the altar in obedience to God and service of our partner is a sacrifice filled with grace and truth—goodness and eternal vision. Our sacrifices are the key to our growth and eternal possibilities.

So it turns out that our sacrifices are not sacrifices, but purchases. We "sacrifice" our puny preferences and God rewards us with eternal joy. What a bargain! In Heaven's economy, so much is gotten for so little!

We often go into marriage under a false premise. During the courtship it seems that we have never had such an effortless way to have fun. Happiness comes so easily. We laugh, giggle, and share from the bottom of our hearts. The satisfactions flow freely.

Yet the full experience of marriage will demand regular payments across time. What seemed so easy at first will later feel impossible. We may feel cheated when we discover that this bargain requires so much of us. Character and companionship do not come without consistent investment. Yet, if we continue to make payments on our relationship, we will be amazed what we get for our "sacrifices."

God knows that what we obtain too easily we esteem too lightly. In His own words, "All those who will not endure chastening, but deny me, cannot be sanctified" (D&C 101:5). To become heavenly, we must endure earthly challenges—including the unexpected ones in marriage.

When Jesus visited America, He told the people that he no longer accepted their sacrifices and burnt offerings. He wanted a new kind of sacrifice. "And ye shall offer for a sacrifice unto me a *broken heart* and a *contrite spirit*" (3 Nephi 9:20, emphasis added).

I feel sure that Jesus is not asking that we be depressed and miserable. I think He is asking that we surrender our demands that things be done our way. In place of being demanding we become agreeable, submissive, cooperative, and appreciative. This is the natural result of allowing Jesus to transform the natural man to the man of Christ.

This change may be most evident in our expectations. Often we hold our partner to some set of mythical standards (which are both unreasonable and unexpressed!). Inevitably he or she falls short. We feel discontent. We judge our companion as flawed and inferior. Over time this subtle discontent grows into the cancerous assurance that our partner is fatally flawed. With time we can easily convince ourselves that the marriage was a mistake.

The cure for cancerous expectations is humble submission—a broken heart and a contrite spirit. This mindset helps us to be better appreciators and more willing learners. If we listen carefully and learn humbly about our partners' points of view, we will be enlarged and enriched.

HEAVENLY "SACRIFICE"

Brigham Young challenged us to think differently about the sacrifices that Heaven demands.

> I have heard a great many tell about what they have suffered for Christ's sake. I am happy to say I never had occasion to. I have enjoyed a great deal, but *so far as suffering goes I have compared it a great many times . . . to a man wearing an old, worn out, tattered and dirty coat, and somebody comes along and gives him one that is new, whole and beautiful.* This is the comparison I draw when I think of what I have suffered for the Gospel's sake—I have thrown away an old coat and have put on a new one. No man or woman ever heard me tell about suffering. "Did you not leave a handsome property in Ohio, Missouri, and Illinois?" Yes. "And have you not suffered through that?" No, I have been growing better and better all the time, and so have this people.[17]

In striking the marriage bargain, we are (unknowingly) giving up the egocentrisms of childhood in favor of the charity of Godhood. We make a covenantal step toward unselfishness. As we progress in marriage we gain ennobled character as well as eternal companionship.

BUYING A HEAVENLY HOME

Heaven draws us toward godliness. Our sacrifices are the paltry down payments on our Heavenly Homes. Making such payments requires faith in the Lord Jesus Christ since the rewards are beyond our view.

Faith is precisely what God wants us to cultivate. "Wherefore, thou shalt do *all that thou doest* in the name of the Son, and thou shalt repent and *call upon God in the name of the Son* forevermore" (Moses 5:8, emphasis added).

We do ALL that we do in the name of the beloved Son. We do it in the spirit of redemptiveness. We do it as a small but meaningful imitation of His sacrifice. We show our willingness to rescue our spouse by giving up our tiny preferences in favor of our spouse's blessing. Such a sacrifice, when graciously made, is full of grace and truth!

Each of us should pray earnestly for the heavenly help to make those sacrifices that will sanctify our relationships. As we enter our homes, we can pause to beseech God to grant us grace, goodness, mercy, compassion, and patience. We can ask Father to help us see our partner and his or her struggles with the loving-kindness with which He views them. In so doing, we place our time, our minds and our hearts on the altar. That is the ultimate offering, the required sacrifice. Making this sacrifice is the heart and soul of the required obedience.

The deed to our heavenly home

In return for Adam and Eve's faith-filled sacrifice, they were rewarded with the Holy Ghost. Such spiritual outpourings must surely be God's way of saying, "I am preparing a place for you. You cannot now imagine the glory. But I assure you, it is grand!"

Adam was taught by the Holy Ghost that "*as thou hast fallen thou mayest be redeemed,* and all mankind, even as many as will" (Moses 5:9, emphasis added).

Notice the beautiful reassurance: We may be redeemed! So can EVERY person who is willing to pay the price. We pay our pennies and dimes. He provides mansions and glory. Wow! What a gracious Paymaster! Adam and Eve clearly understood the magnificence of God's grace. Notice the majesty of their inspired testimonies.

And in that day Adam blessed God and was filled, and began to prophesy concerning all the families of the earth, saying: *Blessed be the name of God,* for because of my transgression my eyes are opened, and *in this life I shall have joy, and again in the flesh I shall see God.*

And Eve, his wife, heard all these things and was *glad,* saying: *Were it not for our transgression we never should have had seed, and never should have known good and evil, and the joy of our redemption, and the eternal life which God giveth unto all the obedient.* (Moses 5:10-11, emphasis added)

Adam and Eve blessed the name of God. Under the inspiration of heaven they recognized His perfect wisdom that placed them in this troubled world and invited them to follow the map of obedience in order to win partnership in God's heavenly enterprise.

In a great parenting side note, the following verse points out how Adam and Eve used their inspired knowledge. "And Adam and Eve blessed the name of God, and *they made all things known unto their sons and their daughters"* (Moses 5:12, emphasis added).

As we know, some of Adam and Eve's children chose to follow in the path of obedience and sacrifice. However, some chose instead to listen to Satan's voice and become fugitives and vagabonds. "And Satan came among them, saying: I am also a son of God; and he commanded them, saying: Believe it not; and they believed it not, and they loved Satan more than God. And men began from that time forth to be carnal, sensual, and devilish" (Moses 5:13).

OBEDIENCE AND SACRIFICE IN MARRIAGE

So the human story began with obedience and sacrifice. The success of our marital story hinges on our willingness to apply the same principles.

Applying these principles to marriage requires inspiration. Obedience entails a willingness to keep the commandments—whether our partner does or not. Obedience means that we love God with all our hearts. Obedience also requires that we "love [our spouse] with all [our] heart, and shalt cleave unto her and none else" (D&C 42:22).

When I think about applying the principle of sacrifice to marriage,

I think of the allegory of a man who had two friends in the manufac-
tured-home business. When he wanted a new house, he asked each
friend to send him half a house. He gave no plans. He provided no spec-
ifications on size or style. He left them to design as they would. So each
friend sent a lovely half-house. When the two halves arrived at the site,
they were jarringly different. Rooms did not line up. Utilities did not
match up. Roofs and walls between the two halves did not connect.

This is a pretty good symbol for marriage. Each of us is created in a
different "factory" or family. Two people come together assuming that
they will readily connect. But we soon find that our traditions, expectations, assumptions, and ways of life do not line up. The more time that
passes, the more clear the differences.

Unfortunately, we apply value judgments to our differences: "Your
family doesn't care about punctuality." "Well, your family doesn't care
about *people.*" Each of us is inclined to believe that the way we have
chosen (or been raised) is the better way. And we are tempted to pull
our half-house down the road until we can find a better match. But we
never match up perfectly with another human being.

What a glorious opportunity for accommodation! God knew that
marriage would provide us unending opportunities to negotiate everything from what's okay to wear on the Sabbath to what spices are
favored in meals. When our relationship is built upon a firm commitment, it can endure—even thrive—in all these negotiations.

Elder Bruce C. Hafen has observed that, "When troubles come, the
parties to a *contractual* marriage seek happiness by walking away. They
marry to obtain benefits and will stay only as long as they're receiving
what they bargained for. But when troubles come to a *covenant* marriage, the husband and wife work them through. They marry to give
and to grow, bound by the covenants to each other, to the community,
and to God."[18]

We covenant to bring all to the altar. The Lord cannot bless what
we will not bring. He asks that we bring our whole souls to Him so that
He can transform us. If we are willing to let Him be the carpenter, He
can blend the two half-houses together. He will help us create new, bet-

ter family traditions and learn to enjoy the spices that our partners enjoy. C. S. Lewis offers a fitting metaphor (drawn from George MacDonald):

> Imagine yourself as a living house. God comes in to rebuild that house. At first, perhaps, you can understand what He is doing. He is getting the drains right and stopping the leaks in the roof and so on: you knew that those jobs needed doing and so you are not surprised. But presently, He starts knock-ing the house about in a way that hurts abominably and does not seem to make sense. What on earth is He up to? The explanation is that He is building quite a different house from the one you thought of—throwing out a new wing here, putting on an extra floor there, running up towers, making courtyards. You thought you were going to be made into a decent little cottage: but He is building a palace.[19]

If we trust the Master Architect and appreciate the style of the other half of our house, God will turn our jarring differences into lovely courtyards and magnificent towers.

A HIGHER KIND OF SUBMISSION

There is a real danger in talk of sacrifice of self and preferences. Godly sacrifice is quite a different thing from the world's kind of submission—giving in and giving up. Passivity is not what God is after. In the world we often encourage people to move from passive compliance to self-respect: "Stand up for yourself!" What we often fail to recognize in the secular world is that there is a level that is still higher than self-respect; it is God-respect. Submitting to God is quite a different thing from being a doormat.

In godly submission, as in all things, Jesus is preeminent. He did not allow Himself to be mocked and crucified because He was weak and frightened. It was a triumph of His goodness that He did not use His immense power to destroy those who persecuted Him. He chose to let goodness govern His power. The Person with the greatest power chose to be the most submissive. There is a lesson there for those who worry about power in the world.

As we imperfect humans develop courage and strength, we don't have to use them to prove ourselves smart or powerful. The better we get, the more we will use our strength to bless. We are "willing to submit to all things which the Lord seeth fit to inflict upon [us], even as a child doth submit to his father" (Mosiah 3:19).

Authors Howard and Kathleen Bahr observed that "self-sacrifice in the service of family members, formerly seen as high virtue, is now often characterized as personality defect or self-defeating behavior. . . . [Yet] the experience of *having* sacrificed, and been sacrificed for—was the essential glue of a moral society. The morality of kinship was a willingness to not 'count the cost' in sacrificing for one's own, in contrast to the morality of the market, which involved contracts, exchange, and profit motives. . . . The morality of the marketplace was ultimately alienating, for it encouraged us to treat people as things and relationships as opportunities for profit."[20]

Sacrifice is generally devalued and misunderstood in our society. Tzvetan Todorov, a social commentator, invites us to think differently: "To care about someone does not mean sacrificing one's time and energy for that person. It means devoting them to the person and taking joy in doing so; in the end, one feels richer for one's efforts, not poorer."[21]

It takes strength of character to see errors in a partner's grammar or perceptions and yet resist the temptation to correct needlessly. It takes godly goodness to see weakness and mistakes in our partners and yet resist the temptation to smirk. It takes heavenly humility to be proven right and yet to meekly acknowledge that we all make mistakes. It takes divine grace to discard or limit the hobbies that prevent us from helping around the house.

Fenelon, a 17th century French Catholic bishop, has captured the sweet spirit of submission in his remarkable prayer:

> Lord, I know not what I ought to ask of thee; Thou only knowest what I need; Thou lovest me better than I know how to love myself. O Father! give to Thy child that which he himself knows

not how to ask. I dare not ask either for crosses or consolations: I simply present myself before Thee, I open my heart to Thee. Behold my needs which I know not myself; see and do according to Thy tender mercy. Smite, or heal; depress me, or raise me up: I adore all thy purposes without knowing them; I am silent; I offer myself in sacrifice; I yield myself to Thee; I would have no other desire than to accomplish Thy will. Teach me to pray. Pray Thyself in me. Amen.[22]

BUILDING CHARACTER THROUGH SACRIFICE

How do we apply this principle to daily irritations? Personal characteristics that we enjoy in some settings become irritations in others. This fact poses a special challenge in marriage. My beloved Nancy is the kindest person I have every known. However, her gentle nature can swamp me with irritation when I want a snap decision. Nancy's kindness is inextricably connected to her gentleness, deliberateness—even indecisiveness. Did I expect God to give me the priceless kindness without asking me to show patience with the indecision? Marriage requires that we do more than tolerate the lesser side of each other's qualities. Over the course of time—even in the best marriages—fundamental, irresolvable differences develop.

For example, in one marriage, *his* unlimited ideas for creative use of money threaten the family's financial well-being and the couple's ultimate retirement. In another, *her* need to spend abundant time with friends leaves *him* feeling unvalued and unloved. Every couple has some fundamental difference that threatens the relationship.

Daniel Wile, a marriage therapist, argues that choosing a partner is choosing a set of problems. "Each potential relationship has its own particular set of inescapable recurring problems. . . . There is value, when choosing a long-term partner, in realizing that you will inevitably be choosing a particular set of unresolvable problems that you'll be grappling with for the next ten, twenty, or fifty years."[23] We can be mad and feel cheated because of those problems. We can move on to another relationship—which will inevitably have its own set of problems. Or we can become experts in dealing with the particular challenges faced in our current relationship.

When we choose the last option, we focus on our own repenting. That is what God recommends. Of course there are relationships that are abusive or destructive and must be ended. Anyone in an abusive relationship should seek wise counseling. If the first counsel you seek does not help you guard your safety, you should seek help from a different counselor.

Relationships that cannot be salvaged are rare. President Joseph Fielding Smith wrote that "if all mankind would live in strict obedience to the gospel, and in that love which is begotten by the Spirit of the Lord, all marriages would be eternal; divorce would be unknown. Divorce is not part of the gospel plan and has been introduced because of the hardness of heart and unbelief of the people. . . . There never could be a divorce in this Church if the husband and wife were keeping the commandments of God."[24]

Most of us suffer garden-variety discontents. When we respond to them with ever-growing irritation, we are serving Satan's purposes. In contrast, God invites us to be like Adam and Eve as we "repent and call upon God in the name of the Son forevermore" (Moses 5:8).

PREPARING FOR REPENTANCE

Repentance is simply the process by which we shed the world's inferior ways and embrace God's superior ways. We discard our worn, tired old garments in favor of God's robes of graciousness.

The process begins when we prepare our hearts. "Thou shalt offer a sacrifice unto the Lord thy God in righteousness, even that of a broken heart and a contrite spirit" (D&C 59:8). Rather than fill ourselves with indignation and demands, we turn to kindness and respect. Doug Brinley has talked about preparing the heart: "When people are upset and angry, they are blind to any position but their own. . . . when people are happy, they communicate adequately. . . . Rather than looking at marriage as a skill issue, let's consider it as a heart matter. *Most adults communicate quite well with other adults when their hearts are soft and they respect one another."* [25]

As we turn our hearts to God, they will be opened to our partners. Turning to our partner's requires us to worry a little less about our own needs. As Howard and Kathleen Bahr observe: "The careful attention to self necessary to assure that the self is not sacrificing more than his share, that he is caring for himself 'well,' means that his attention cannot be fully focused on the needs of the other." [26] We cannot have our eyes on our partner and ourselves at the same time. The Bahrs further observe that "people's needs are inconvenient; they are not ordered according to an eight-hour day divided by coffee and lunch breaks." [27] A godly approach to marriage will entail inconvenience and sacrifice.

Next, we prepare our minds. As Elder Boyd K. Packer reminds us: "It was meant to be that life would be a challenge. To suffer some anxiety, some depression, some disappointment, even some failure is normal. Teach our members that if they have a good, miserable day once in a while, or several in a row, to stand steady and face them. Things will straighten out. There is great purpose in our struggle in life." [28]

Rather than see difficulties as some form of unfairness, we can see them as a normal part of life and as a heavenly invitation to growth. Elder Dallin H. Oaks teaches us that "through the lens of spirituality we see all the commandments of God as invitations to blessings. Obedience and sacrifice, loyalty and love, fidelity and family, all appear in eternal perspective." [29]

Mapping the future

Part of preparing our minds requires us to anticipate the challenges we will face, and committing ourselves to respond in new and better ways. By reviewing the past we can anticipate what relationship challenges we will face in the days ahead. We can mentally project forward to a scene that has usually caused distress. We can see ourselves reacting in the old way, choose to place our desires on the altar, and beg God to purify them.

Then we make a new plan. We bring faith, obedience and sacrifice to the planning. We ask God to show us how we can respond more as He would have us. We can mentally rehearse the new reaction. Most of us need to rehearse it many times to be ready to act in different ways.

Try as we might, we won't do it perfectly right away. We will be distracted by ego, tripped by pride, snared by temper, or sidetracked by pain. So we go through the process again. We may need to apologize and ask our spouse for patience as we learn to do better.

I have been trying to be a better spouse for more than 30 years. I still have a long way to go. I still say the smart-alecky comment that doesn't help. I still fume when my needs aren't met or I am inconvenienced. But those things happen less than they used to. More often Nancy and I are so happy, we are amazed. In our experience it is just as God promises: "Give, and it shall be given unto you; good measure, pressed down, and shaken together, and running over, shall men give into your bosom. For with the same measure that ye mete withal it shall be measured to you again" (Luke 6:38).

As you finish this chapter, I invite you to respond to the questions and suggestions at the end. I call these exercises "Creating Your Own Story" since each of us has the opportunity of designing our own thoughts, feelings, and actions. Test these ideas and activities in the laboratory of your marriage.

Creating Your Own Story

Sometimes we imagine a tidy set of skills that will enable us to process our partnership woes effectively. But good marriage is not about skills. It is about character. Consider your thoughts, feelings, and actions that are the measure of your character—and the key factors in a godly relationship.

Thoughts

What are some things your partner says or does that get under your skin? How can you see those same things positively? How can you discover your own assumptions or expectations and enjoy his or her way of doing things?

What are the qualities that first attracted you to your partner? What additional qualities have you discovered over the period of your relationship? What can you do to keep the good qualities at the front of your mind? Would it help to make a list and keep it with you? Would it be useful to have pictures of best times on your desk or in your wallet?

Feelings

Do you notice when feelings of irritation are growing in you? What can you do to purge the irritation? Does it help to take a few minutes for a quiet prayer for heavenly mercy? Do you have a relaxation routine (exercise, relaxation, deep breathing) that can help you settle down when hard feelings are festering?

When you want to increase the positives in your relationship, try remembering great moments in your relationship history and rehearse them in your mind. In an ideal situation you might relax, close your eyes, and re-live the good experience. Occasionally, you might page through your photo album or journal to remind you of good times you may have forgotten.

Actions

What principle of the gospel do you feel invited to live more fully?

What can you do for your partner that would be an appreciated sacrifice? Can you listen more intently, help more with household tasks, or withhold judgment and show greater kindness? Can you set aside or reduce golf, videogames, shopping, primping, or T.V. watching? What activity would you be willing to give up in order to strengthen your relationship? In some ways this may feel like you are leaving the Garden of Eden and entering the lone and dreary world. However, the willingness to make wise sacrifices and make them gladly opens the doors to understanding heaven's purposes—just as with Adam and Eve.

Consider setting your mind and heart to act lovingly toward your partner. Stretch yourself to do that longer than you have in the past whether an hour, a day, a week, or a month. Make up your mind to see your partner positively and to act kindly.

NOTES

15 *Journal of Discourses.* Edited by George D. Watt, et al. 26 vols. Liverpool: F. D. Richards, et al., [1854-1886], 24:197-98.

16 Harry Emerson Fosdick, *The Meaning of Faith,* New York: Association Press [1918], 20, emphasis added.

17 John A. Widstoe, *Discourses of Brigham Young,* Salt Lake City: Deseret Book, [1973], 348, emphasis added.

18 Douglas E. Brinley and D. K. Judd (Eds.), *Living in a Covenant Marriage,* Salt Lake City: Deseret Book [2004], 1.

19 *Mere Christianity,* New York: Macmillan [1960], 174.

20 Howard M. & Kathleen S. Bahr, "Families and Self-sacrifice: Alternative Models and Meanings for Family Theory," *Social Forces,* [2001], Journal #79:1231.

21 *Facing the Extreme Moral Life in the Concentration Camps,* New York: Metropolitan Books, [1996], 85-86.

22 Francois de la Mothe Fenelon quoted in Harry Emerson Fosdick, *Meaning of Prayer,* 58-59.

23 *After the Honeymoon: How Conflict Can Improve Your Relationship,* New York: Wiley [1988], 13.

24 *Living in a Covenant Marriage,* 11.

25 *Covenant Marriage,* 25-26, emphasis in original.

26 *Social Forces,* 1245-46.

27 *Social Forces,* 1250.

28 "Solving Emotional Problems in the Lord's Own Way," *Ensign,* May 1978, 93.

29 *Pure in Heart,* 123.

CHAPTER THREE

FAITH IN THE LORD JESUS CHRIST:

"Lord I believe; help thou mine unbelief."

SETTING THE STAGE

Think of reasons you are grateful to the Lord Jesus Christ. Do you feel blessed by His amazing life and example? Do you feel Him sustaining you from moment to moment by lending you breath? Do you recognize the incomparable gift of His sacrifice to redeem your soul? Do you "stand all amazed" that He went beyond paying for your sins to bear your pains and sorrows so that His compassion would be fully activated? Do you feel you would join that obscure woman in washing His feet with your tears if you were given the chance?

REPLACING EVIL WITH GOODNESS

Jesus was just returning with Peter, James, and John from the transcendent experience on the Mount of Transfiguration. Together they had been visited and taught by God, Moses and Elijah. They had their eyes on Eternity. Then they descended from Heavenly communion to earthly contention. They ran into the jarring scene of Jesus' disciples contending with a group of scribes. Jesus asked the scribes about the subject of their contention. They dared not answer him. However, "one of the multitude answered and said, Master, I have brought unto

47

thee my son, which hath a dumb spirit" (Mark 9:17).

The man who spoke came as an anxious and desperate father. We can hear the tender concern in his voice. "And wheresoever he [the evil spirit] taketh him, he teareth him: and he foameth, and gnasheth with his teeth, and pineth away: and I spake to thy disciples that they should cast him out; and they could not" (Mark 9:18).

His apostles had previously been given the power to cast out devils. They had previously performed miracles. But they had no success with this man's son. Jesus identified the reason they were unsuccessful. It was a *lack of faith*. Had their faith faltered as Jesus and the leading apostles were away? Did the power fail them because they depended on themselves rather than God? Had they become careless in regard to drawing heavenly power into their ministering?

Jesus called for the boy to be brought to Him. The evil spirit in the boy perceived Jesus to be an enemy and the boy immediately exploded into convulsions. Jesus asked the father how long the boy had been troubled by the terrible seizures. "From childhood," was the father's reply. Jesus did not ask because He did not know—He knew and knows all things. He asked so that His disciples could understand that even the most intractable enemies have no power in the face of Heavenly Authority.

Again we hear the father's soul-rending cry as he describes his son's suffering: "And ofttimes it hath cast him into the fire, and into the waters, to destroy him: but if thou canst do any thing, have compassion on us, and help us" (Mark 9:22). This broken-hearted father would do anything to rescue his son from Satan's grasp.

The man posed the question whether Jesus could do anything: "If thou canst do anything . . .." Jesus reversed the challenge: "If thou canst believe, all things are possible to him that believeth" (Mark 9:23). The question is not whether Jesus is able to heal. The question is whether we will believe in Him.

The father's response was poignant. "And straightway the father of the child cried out, and said with tears, Lord, I believe; help thou mine unbelief" (Mark 9:24). (How often we are all in the same dilemma as the father. "Lord, I believe. I want to believe. I'm trying to believe. Will you give life to my imperfect efforts to believe?")

The father's faltering efforts to believe were enough. Jesus responded with power: "He rebuked the foul spirit, saying unto him, Thou dumb and deaf spirit, I charge thee, come out of him, and enter no more into him" (Mark 9:25). Jesus gladly dispatches the evil from all our lives—when our faith—even our budding faith—invites Him.

After the evil spirit departed, the boy collapsed and appeared quite dead. In fact, we often appear quite dead when evil departs. We may be inclined to say, "What's left?" Life may seem empty and we may feel quite listless even as we are relieved of the evil that bedevils us.

"But Jesus took him by the hand, and lifted him up; and he arose" (Mark 9:27). Just as He does with us. He takes us by the hand, lifts us up, and we arise to new life.

It is not enough to cast out evil. We need more. We have vibrant, light-filled life when Jesus lifts us up. And Jesus lifts us up when we focus our souls on Him.

In this great story Jesus taught all of His followers that it takes focused faith to remove the most stubborn and persistent maladies of mortality. It takes faith in the Lord Jesus Christ to remove evil from our marriages and bring them to vibrant life.

PUT GOD FIRST

President Ezra Taft Benson taught us that "when we put God first, all other things fall into their proper place or drop out of our lives. Our love of the Lord will govern the claims for our affection, the demands on our time, the interests we pursue, and the order of our priorities. We should put God ahead of everyone else in our lives."[30] That's a powerful idea: When we put God first, everything else falls into its proper place!

But how does all this relate to the frictions and challenges of marriage? Can faith in the Lord Jesus Christ make a difference in the quality of our relationships?

FAITH IN THE LORD JESUS CHRIST
PROVIDES ETERNAL PERSPECTIVE

Marriage is full of tempests in teapots. We bristle over our partner's word choice or disinterest in our story. We fret and complain about this purchase or that insensitivity. We grumble about a chore neglected or a kindness unappreciated. We may be bothered by indecisiveness, hygiene, grammar, food preferences, clothing style, personality, lack of religiosity, stubbornness . . . the list is endless! Over time we transform irritations into evils. With time we come to think of our partners as disappointments or failures.

On the way to work one day Nancy asked me a question. I gave a carefully-considered answer. She looked perplexed and asked me to repeat my answer. I growled at her. I felt the indignation that is so human: "Why didn't you listen to what I said?"

It was all very natural. Very human. Later in the day I felt guilty. I knew I had done wrong. I probably had given a reasonable answer to her question. But Nancy may have been thinking about something else. She may have been distracted as I was explicating. The irony is that I do the same thing to her all the time. I'm distracted as she answers my question and I ask her to repeat her answer.

Why is that forgivable when I am inattentive, but not when Nancy is? The answer is pride. I see the whole world from the perspective of my needs, wants, and preferences. That is the painful reality of humanness.

The irony—or one among many ironies—is that Nancy and I were talking about arranging a visit to our home by a pest control man. We have chiggers and ticks in our backyard. But, even worse than those pests, I have judgment and narrowness in my soul. (I wonder if they can spray for those.) I believe that if we replace judgment and condemnation of each other with compassion and love, we not only find more peace, serenity, and tranquility but also become one smidgen more like God.

Nancy and I have lots of faults. At least I do. Yet we enjoy each other immeasurably almost all the time! So I testify of the power of faith. It causes us to be a little more patient with temporary—but annoying—humanness.

When our focus is on the unpleasant and mundane, we trivialize everything. We become like the three stooges, endlessly punching and shoving each other. What a shame for nobles who are on a journey Home to the King! Like those in Zion's Camp on the journey to redeem Missouri, we bicker and bristle and fail to claim the blessings that God has offered.

Is our faith a vibrant and ennobling power in our lives? Or do our complaints and discomforts eclipse any vision of the eternal? An acquaintance once described to me his philosophy, life as pointless tragedy: "It is our duty to suffer and die for the amusement of our creator. And I'm doing my part." Jesus taught something far nobler: Life as perfectly-guided moral education.

For the Latter-day Saints, God has opened visions of eternity. We have seen His face in the glorious Latter-day theology. We have felt His relentless redemptiveness in the great plan of happiness.

Satan knows that faith in the Lord Jesus Christ and His redemptiveness are enemies to his cause. Satan's best hope is to keep us from looking up. He must keep us fully absorbed with the trivial, fretting over our inconveniences and stewing over our grievances.

Brigham Young was once approached by two sisters, each of whom wanted a divorce. I paraphrase his response: "If you could only see your husband as he will be in the glorious resurrection, this very husband you now say you despise, your first impulse would be to kneel and worship him."[31] He said the same thing to husbands who had "fallen out of love" with their wives. Those are mighty words.

When we have the eternal perspective on our marriages, everything is different. Filled with faith, we might adapt Jesus' advice as our mantra: "Look unto me in every thought; doubt not, fear not" (D&C 6:36). I would add "fret not, panic not."

We can even go one step farther. When we have vibrant faith in the Lord Jesus Christ, we know that the irritations and challenges of marriage are blessings intended to develop our character. As Elder Jeffrey R. Holland observed, "Too often too many of us run from the very things that will bless us and save us and soothe us. Too often we see gospel commitments and commandments as something to be feared and forsaken."[32]

As we turn from the ways of the natural man to the ways of Christ, we will respond to our challenges differently. Instead of judging our partner, we will invite Christ to soften our hearts and fill us with goodness. No challenges or differences in marriage can thwart the work of God-given charity.

Carlfred Broderick, a nationally respected Marriage and Family Therapist, told of a sister who appeared to have brought family misery on herself and her children-to-be by her choice in husbands. Soon after a temple marriage, the husband quit the Church and, as the children joined their family, he lured them into his faith-deprived lifestyle. It appeared that all four of their children would choose non-spiritual and non-religious lives. When Broderick was called upon to give her a blessing as her stake president, he made a great discovery. The Lord revealed to him that this good woman had chosen to take these trials as part of her covenant to rescue some of God's children who would struggle in mortality. This woman should be commended rather than judged. With the help of a good bishop, the older son chose to serve a mission and he joined his mother in bringing a spiritual influence to the family. What appeared to be an unwise woman was a savior on Mount Zion.[33]

President Howard W. Hunter taught us that "whatever Jesus lays his hands upon lives. If Jesus lays his hands upon a marriage, it lives. If he is allowed to lay his hands on the family, it lives."[34]

FAITH IN THE LORD JESUS CHRIST
POINTS US OUTWARD

Elder Hafen has described three kinds of wolves that test every marriage. The first is the adversity that is a part of mortality. The second is our own imperfections. He describes the third as the "excessive individualism" that causes us to evaluate everything in terms of its effect on us. The value of every experience and every person is based on whether they meet our needs and honor our preferences.[35]

When we have this mindset we are like the person described by

Thomas Clayton Wolfe: "Poor, dismal, ugly, sterile, shabby little man...with your scrabble of harsh oaths...Joy, glory, and magnificence were here for you...but you scrabbled along...rattling a few stale words... and would have none of them."[36]

The gospel of Jesus Christ is designed to lift our vision from our own petty and relentless wants to something nobler. "Every man seeking the interest of his neighbor, and doing all things with an eye single to the glory of God" (D&C 82:19).

Bart Benson tells of being called upon to give marriage counsel when he was a just a young man serving as a missionary and branch president in Venezuela. A ward member had joined the church over the objections of his wife. Every time they tried to discuss the subject, she became angry. The man sought counsel from the young, untrained, and inexperienced missionary.

> I opened my mouth to spout some platitudes of comfort and hope, but instead an idea crowded them out and expressed itself. For once my broken Spanish was clear and unencumbered.
>
> "My friend," I began, "next time you and your wife begin to discuss your baptism and you start to feel anger and frustration, stop. Say no more for a moment. Then take your wife into your arms, and hold her tight. Tell her that you love her, you appreciate her, and nothing will take her place in your life."
>
> He looked at me blankly. Perhaps he had expected a lecture or some grand principle that would save his marriage. He waited, maybe expecting me to continue, but I had nothing else to say. . . .
>
> "Yes, Presidente," he said. He left my office solemnly without saying anything more.
>
> A week passed, and once again Fernando walked into the chapel. But there was a lightness in his step. His head was up, his eyes were clear, and he smiled. Throughout the meeting he fidgeted like a small child. Afterward he came to my office.
>
> "Presidente, Presidente!" he exclaimed in a quiet but excited voice. "You will not believe what happened. I did as you said. We talked again of my faith and my baptism. Again she criticized me and told

me I was deceived. I wanted to yell and tell her she was wrong, but I remembered your words. I stopped, took a breath, and looked at her, trying to remember all the years of love we have shared and the love that I still feel. She must have felt something in my gaze, for she softened. I took her into my arms and held her. I whispered that I love her, that I appreciate her, and that nothing could take her place as my wife. We cried. Then, sitting close, we talked for many hours about all we have experienced—the good, the bad—and then I held her again. For the first time in many weeks we felt love. Thank you, Presidente."[37]

When we are in disagreement in a marriage, very often our focus is on persuading our partner that we are right. This is much like trying to grab something from a child. As surely as we grab, the child will resist. As surely as we try to take from our partner her or his beliefs and preferences, we will get resistance and defensiveness.

When we try to drag our partners to our view of the world, they kick, fight, and scream. When, in contrast, we invite our partners to gaze with us on truths of eternity, we are more likely to find common ground. When we choose to love and appreciate our partners in spite of our differences, we open the door to love. When Fernando chose to focus on their common love rather than his own religious discoveries, he and his wife could move forward together.

President Gordon B. Hinckley has counseled us about the danger of focus on self in marriage: "I find selfishness to be the root cause of most of [the problems that lead to broken homes]. I am satisfied that a happy marriage is not so much a matter of romance as it is an anxious concern for the comfort and well-being of one's companion. . . . There is a remedy for all of this. It is not found in divorce. It is found in the gospel of the Son of God. He it was who said, 'What therefore God hath joined together, let not man put asunder' (Matthew 19:6). The remedy for most marriage stress is not in divorce. It is in repentance. It is not in separation. It is in simple integrity that leads a man to square up his shoulders and meet his obligations. It is found in the Golden Rule."[38]

Faith in the Lord Jesus Christ requires that we trust that God is working to rescue our spouses even as He is working to rescue us. When we have energizing faith in Christ, we trust His progress with our partner. The more we trust God's purposes in perfecting our partners (and don't try to take over the job ourselves), the more we all progress.

As Elder David A. Bednar said at BYU, "I wonder if we ever learn to acknowledge our daily dependence upon the enabling power of the Atonement."[39] We cannot have great marriages without His participation.

FAITH IN THE LORD JESUS CHRIST
ASSURES US THAT WE ARE NOT LIVING A GAME OF CHANCE

As marital irritations accumulate, it is easy to imagine that our marital choice was a hormone-sodden mistake. We forget the affirmations that pushed us toward marriage. We begin to honor instead our pre-marital doubts and vacillation. We might even begin to believe, as a friend in a troubled marriage once said to me: "This marriage is a punishment for my youthful impulsiveness."

In the grip of such delusions, it seems necessary—even wise—to quit the relationship and start over. "I'll do better the second time." "My life might be so much better if I had just chosen differently" or "It wouldn't be that big of a deal if I blew out of this marriage and into one with a better person—perhaps God might even want that for me." This is Satan at work.

As an almost universal rule, the best course is to honor covenants. One of the best-kept secrets in this world is that troubled, painful relationships can become both satisfying and growth-promoting as we fill ourselves with faith in God and love for His purposes. To quit a relationship because it is difficult is like dropping out of school because a course is so much harder and requires so much more of you than you expected.

It is hard to rightly express the truth about God's influence in our lives. I believe the truth is something close to: "If I am trying to live the gospel, God will not allow anything to happen to me that cannot become a blessing for me." Of course there is a little trick in this formulation. God can turn almost any of our choices into blessings. He has an amazing ability to transform our bad decisions into growth. But I believe it is also true that he even rescues us from having to face or confront decisions if we are not prepared for them. He keeps us from challenges that we cannot reasonably conquer.

As a loving parent, our perfect Father will help us in a multitude of ways to avoid ruining our lives and pre-empting our growth unless we simply defy Him.

A vital part of the truth is that God can take our messed-up lives and transform them into purposeful growth. Our choices in partners are not just random events in our lives. With our limited view, it's reasonable to question if we might have bettered ourselves by choosing differently. Yet God is orchestrating our lives to a greater extent than we appreciate. Faith invites us to honor covenants and not jettison a relationship because of continuing troubles. God honors those who honor their covenants.

A dear and respected friend called me once to ask, "Can I quit this marriage yet?" His wife had turned her back on him and on the Church. There appeared to be nothing that could be done to rescue the relationship. Could he file for divorce yet? My answer was that, when we understand covenants, we do everything we are able. We don't pull the plug.

This good man returned to giving his best to the relationship. His wife continued her path and eventually left the relationship. Yet he knew that he had given his best.

When we have vibrant faith, we trust that God brought us together for a good reason. We trust that He will refine and perfect us if we keep trying. We trust that all things work together for good for them that trust Him. We trust that we will one day be happier together than we can imagine.

This is the perspective of faith. It acknowledges that our lives are not random or meaningless.

Brigham Young said, "There is not a single condition of life that is entirely unnecessary; there is not one hour's experience but what is beneficial to all those who make it their study, and aim to improve upon the experience they gain."[40]

At times of relationship stress the best of us may wonder if we should have married differently—if we made a mistake. My guess is that, in ways not discerned by us, God guided us to be together. My guess is that God can take our marital choices and make them ideally suited to bless and balance us. At my best I am the perfect man for Nancy. Nancy at her best is the perfect partner for me. I believe that. In fact I believe that God guides our lives in ways that we almost never discern. Not only does He sustain us from moment to moment by lending us breath, He also guides, rescues, protects, teaches, and blesses constantly.

With that belief as context, I think that one of Satan's fundamental objectives is to undermine that sense. He wants us to think our lives are random or full of mistakes. I believe that any time we are trying to serve God, He protects us in numberless ways.

If I'm right, the idea has important consequences. It means that we should put our thinking and acting in service *not only* of the covenants we have made but also of the blessings God has brought into our lives. For example, any time we feel irritated with each other it is an opportunity to grow. Irritation is an invitation to better thinking and acting. Since, in most cases, we are perfectly designed for each other, staying engaged with each other is vital. But it isn't a matter of stubborn resolve. It is a matter of replacing irritation with compassion and charity; replacing accusation with humility; replacing frustration with invitation.

Satan wants us to believe that our commitments (such as marriage partner) are chance events. That way we have no responsibility to repent. We simply re-make the decision. We move to a new marriage. It makes perfect sense—perfect telestial sense. However, serial monogamy often means failed growth.

God has other designs. He has hooked us up with partners and life experiences that are perfectly suited to grow us toward godhood. Rather than run from repentance, He wants us to embrace it. Every time we are inclined to drop out of a life commitment, God is inviting us to solve the unpleasant chafing by becoming more like Him.

One of the neat implications of this line of reasoning is that it gives us guidance for all our feeling, thinking, and acting. When we feel any level of irritation, God is saying, "Hey! Here's a chance for you to become more like me!" In any miserable relationship we can remain "a feverish, selfish little clod of ailments and grievances complaining that the world will not devote itself to making you happy" (George Bernard Shaw) or we can repent and move one step closer to being like Him.

President Hunter invited us to this kind of faith: "I am aware that life presents many challenges, but with the help of the Lord, we need not fear. If our lives and our faith are centered on Jesus Christ and his restored gospel, nothing can ever go permanently wrong. On the other hand, if our lives are not centered on the Savior and his teachings, no other success can ever be permanently right."[41]

JESUS' UNIQUE QUALIFICATION

Faith in the Lord Jesus Christ can transform our imperfect relationships into purposeful growth and soul-filling companionship. It is the foundation on which strong relationships are built.

When the floods and storms of life assail us, and we begin to sink, we can call on Him as Peter did: "While [Peter's] eyes were fixed upon the Lord, the wind could toss his hair and the spray could drench his robes, but all was well—he was coming to Christ. Only when his faith and his focus wavered, only when he removed his glance from the Master to see the furious waves and the black gulf beneath him, only then did he begin to sink. In fear he cried out, "Lord, save me."[42]

My great grandmother died years before I was born, but I feel that I know her well. My dad has told me about her, and I have read her history. Grandma had a very hard life. She raised eleven children with very little support and very little money. There were only two things she hated: alcohol and sheep. You can probably guess some things about her husband. He was a sheepherder with a drinking problem.

With all the demands of life, Grandma did not enjoy the luxury of leisure time. She looked forward to the time when her children were raised so she could have time to read and to sew. She saved to buy a cherished book.

Then the children were raised. Finally she had time! And she went blind. The irony is almost too cruel. Dad has told me about going to visit her and asking her, as she sat in her chair, how she was doing. Her answer echoes through our family history. Though she could have been bitter, her stock answer was, "I'm all right. I'm all right."

Grandma endured mortal disappointments—and did it faithfully and cheerfully—because she trusted in God's ability to turn experience into blessings. She did not enjoy satisfying companionship in mortality, yet she trusted God to reward her faithfulness in eternity.

Having faith does not make everything easy. Rather, faith makes life and its challenges both bearable and meaning-filled.

Postscript

Reflect on the peace and optimism you have felt when you have been filled with His goodness. Our best decisions are those that are made when we are filled with that love and goodness.

Creating Your Own Story

Sometimes we get buried in the here and now. Jesus invites us to look to eternity. We can lift our eyes from daily irritations to heavenly purposes and eternal joys.

Thoughts

Spouses unchanged by the Spirit of God are likely to find fault with many things their partners say and do. This tendency can be replaced by a much more helpful one. When our partners say or do things that surprise or bother us, we can begin a friendly investigation. In our own minds we can ask ourselves, "I wonder why he feels or acts that way?" "I wonder why that is important to her?" Rather than judging our partners, we can seek to understand them.

Feelings

Many of us occasionally get discouraged with our personal spiritual progress. The best remedies for such discouragement are projects and people. When we get busy doing things that we do well, we feel better. When we are around people who enjoy us, we feel better. What projects and people can you draw into your life to lift your spirits?

Sometimes our spirits are burdened by the challenges and disappointments of life and marriage. In both arenas, we can make a conscious choice to cast our burdens on the Lord. We can trust His perfect purposes. When doubt and anxiety arise, we can call on Him to keep us safe. We can remember that He is able to do His redemptive work. He is able to repair hearts and relationships that seem irreparable to us.

Actions

Our spouses also feel burdened from time to time. Sometimes they seem cranky—but they may be quietly carrying pain and loneliness. Rather than respond to our partner's negativity with our own negativity, we can invite them to greater closeness and peacefulness when we offer persuasion, long-suffering, gentleness, meekness, and love unfeigned (See D&C 121:41).

Notes

30   "The Great Commandment—Love the Lord," *Ensign,* May 1988, 4, emphasis in original.

31   Truman Madsen, "The Temple and the Atonement," *Meridian Magazine online,* July 28, 2003.

32   *Trusting Jesus* [2003], 74.

33   Carlfred Broderick, "The Uses of Adversity," in *The Best of Women's Conference,* Salt Lake City: Bookcraft [2000], 50-66.

34   "Reading the Scriptures," *Ensign,* Nov. 1979, 65.

35   Douglas E. Brinley and D. K. Judd (Eds.), *Living in a Covenant Marriage,* Salt Lake City: Deseret Book [2004], 3.

36   Laurence J. Peters, *Peter's Quotations: Ideas for Our Time,* New York: Bantam [1977], 6.

37   Bart Benson, "Unexpected Marriage Advice," *Ensign,* Aug. 2005, 68.

38   "What God Hath Joined Together," *Ensign,* May 1991, 73-74.

39   "In the Strength of the Lord," *Brigham Young University 2001-2002 Devotional and Fireside Speeches,* 7.

40   *Journal of Discourses,* 9:292.

41   Howard W. Hunter, *The Teachings of Howard W. Hunter,* Salt Lake City: Bookcraft [1997], 40.

42   Jeffrey R. Holland, *Trusting Jesus,* Salt Lake City: Deseret Book [2003], 75.

Chapter Four

Humility and Repentance:

"O Jesus, thou Son of God, have mercy on me."

Nancy and I have good friends whose marriage is probably typical of many. Occasionally the husband gets irritated and begins to carp on his wife's faults and limitations. "Why isn't the house clean?" "Why haven't the kids done their chores?" "When will dinner be ready?" The wife bore the nagging as long as she could. On one occasion she grew weary and reacted, "You know, you have faults too!" And the husband replied, "Yes. But they don't bother me like yours do!"

This is precisely the wrong strategy for strengthening a relationship. It assumes that my needs are to be met—and my spouse must do whatever is necessary to assure that they are met. This is the opposite of humility and repentance. It is the enemy of love.

The marker for pride

God has graciously given each of us an early warning system. When we are feeling irked, annoyed, or irritated with our spouse, we have our backs toward heaven. We are guilty of pride. In a spiritual sense we are saying to our spouses, "You are not meeting my needs the way I would like them met. Don't you realize that is your job?! Your every act is to be dedicated to my happiness. *Now hop to it!*"

Pride is burdensome.

THE MORAL INVERSION

The natural man is inclined to love himself and fix others. God has asked us to do the opposite. We are to fix *ourselves* by repenting, and to love *others*. It is not surprising that we have difficulties in marriage. We so often do the very things that will destroy our relationships.

In great literature—including scripture—the highest and noblest service entailed sacrifice and selflessness. In contrast, evil was always self-centered and self-serving.

Today's culture teaches a very different lesson from traditional wisdom: We now hear that it is noble and worthy to focus on our own needs. It is our first obligation. Roy Baumeister, a penetrating and contemporary social psychologist, has observed:

> Morality has become allied with self-interest. It is not simply that people have the right to do what is best for themselves; rather, it has become an almost sacred obligation to do so. The modern message is that what is right and good and valuable to do in life is to focus on yourself, to learn what is inside you, to express and cultivate these inner resources, to do what is best for yourself, and so forth.

> Many Americans today can no longer accept the idea that love requires
> sacrificing oneself or making oneself unhappy or doing things that do not (at least eventually) serve one's individual best interests. If a relationship does not bring pleasure, insight, satisfaction, and fulfillment to the self, then it is regarded as wrong, and the individual is justified–perhaps even obligated–to   end the relationship and find a new, more fulfilling one. According to today's values, "A kind of selfishness is essential to love."[43]

The modern dilemma is ironic. We are devoted to finding happiness—and we are seeking happiness in ways that guarantee emptiness. To the modern mind, it doesn't make logical "sense" that if we sacrifice our own wants and needs, in favor of our spouse's, that we will find true joy and happiness. It takes faith to believe that "he that loseth his life for my sake shall find it" (Matt. 10:39). Without that foundational faith, it's tempting to do what seems to makes sense—and that is to look after ourselves and tend toward selfishness.

When we have tossed sacrifice, obligation, and unselfishness from our contributions to relationships, we have nothing left but an empty egocentrism. We do not have the humility to repent. And, without repentance, there is neither growth nor redemption.

THE MENTAL INVERSION

Our fundamental mortal wiring works against our progress and happiness—especially in the way we think. Psychologists tell us that we are all naive realists, which causes all of us to acknowledge that we all have limited facts and active biases. No human sees clearly. (But I do.) "Each of us thinks we see the world directly, as it really is. If [others] don't agree, it follows either that they have not yet been exposed to the relevant facts or else that they are blinded by their interests and ideologies. . . . Everyone is influenced by ideology and self-interest. Except for me. I see things as they are."[44]

The natural mind is an enemy to truth. Each one of us sees our own versions of "truth" and imagines that no one in the world sees truth as clearly as we do. This way of thinking is a pernicious enemy. It keeps each of us from connecting with others and from being taught by God. Satan laughs.

Satan will laugh us into conflict and misunderstanding—unless we yield to the enticings of the Holy Spirit and put off the natural man (see Mosiah 3:19). No wonder God asks us to become as children—submissive, meek, humble, patient, full of love, willing to submit to all things. Unless we submit ourselves to God and His extraordinary way of thinking, we will always be isolated and discontented.

Humility is the friend of truth. Humility opens us up to the experience of others and to truth from heaven. Humility requires not only that we believe in God, that He is all-wise and all-powerful, but also that "man doth not comprehend all the things which the Lord can comprehend" (Mosiah 4:9). We must set aside our provincial view of the world (and of our spouses), and be open to our partner's perspective. We must invite truth, the heavenly perspective.

As Terrance Olson, faculty member at BYU, has observed, "the quality of emotions we experience is different when we are faithful and humble as compared to when we live without faith and with the kind of arrogance that makes us independent of God."[45] Turning to God in faith and repentance is the cure for pride and self-centeredness.

RECONCILABLE DIFFERENCES

Andy Christensen and Neil Jacobson are therapists and researchers who have studied the process of marital misunderstanding.[46] Their insights are penetrating. They remind us just how human we are—with all that entails. I have summarized their description of the pattern of marital misunderstanding—combined with my own spiritual commentary.

The scene is set for the battle because of our pride. Pride includes our own attunement to our own needs as the standard of judgment. Pride also includes the fact that we honestly believe that we understand our partners and what makes them tick. We presume to understand their thoughts, motives and intent better than even they themselves do.

Preparation for battle then begins in earnest. In our minds we review our partners' violations of good will. And we analyze their characters and study our histories for other violations.

Notice how the pride continues. We define the problem—whatever it is—in terms of our partner. And we tell the story to ourselves in ways that suggest we were earnestly and innocently going about life when our partners hurt us. We are innocent. They are guilty. Our narrow focus keeps us from noticing our own gaps in knowledge, our personal failings as well as the good qualities and good intentions of our partners.

So we enter battle prepared to whack off the offending behaviors and traits in our partners. But our partners respond to the attacks with counter-offensives. The story our partners tell is very different from ours—filled with *their* innocence and *our* errors. We respond with indignation and fury. The battle is on.

While Satan laughs at every step of this dismal process, he must take special delight when people who have promised to bless and encourage each other throw their best efforts into hurting and defeating each other.

We leave each battle dismayed that our partners did not see our wisdom and respond with needed changes. And, hunched over a lonely campfire, we continue to grieve over our injuries and rehearse our opponents' offences.

Christensen and Jacobson suggest that one fundamental problem with this sad script is that it is based on the premise that our partner should change. They suggest that acceptance may be more important than change in strong marriages. (More about this in Chapter 7)

LEARNING FROM THOSE WHO DID IT RIGHT

If we want to move from spiritual anemia to spiritual power, we should learn from those scriptural models who have done that very thing. My personal favorite is Alma. He went from being among the vilest of sinners (Mosiah 28:4) and racked with torment (Alma 36:12) to experiencing inexpressible joy (Alma 36:21) and the presence of God (Alma 36:22) within only a few hours! Wow! What was his magical process?

Alma was only a beginner in faith—he merely remembered his father prophesying about a Son of God who would come to atone for the sins of the world (Alma 36:17). But in the depths of his struggle, he did something with as much sincerity and absolute trust as anyone in the history of this troubled world: He threw himself completely on the merits and mercy of Jesus. "Now, as my mind caught hold upon this thought, I cried within my heart: O Jesus, thou Son of God, have mercy on me, who am in the gall of bitterness, and am encircled about by the everlasting chains of death" (Alma 36:18).

He knew that his ONLY hope was outside of himself. He knew that, if he was going to be saved, Jesus was going to have to do it. And that is the repentance paradox. In order to be saved, we must stop trying to save ourselves by our own power. We must turn ourselves over to Christ completely. That is what Alma did particularly well.

In describing his change to his son Shiblon, Alma said:

And it came to pass that I was three days and three nights in the most bitter pain and anguish of soul; and *never, until I did cry out unto the Lord Jesus Christ for mercy, did I receive a remission of my sins.* But behold, I did cry unto him and I did find peace to my soul.

And now, my son, I have told you this that ye may learn wisdom, that ye may learn of me that there is *no other way or means whereby man can be saved, only in and through Christ.* Behold, he is the life and the light of the world. Behold, he is the word of truth and righteousness. (Alma 38:8-9, emphasis added)

It is perfectly clear from Alma's writings that this dependence on God does not excuse us from doing all that we are able. There is, however, a key difference between our usual way of trying to obey and Alma's way: he turned his life over to God, holding nothing back. He had no illusions about his ability to save himself. Perhaps this is the central doctrine of the Book of Mormon. Nephi's classic words are: "And we talk of Christ, we rejoice in Christ, we preach of Christ, we prophesy of Christ, and we write according to our prophecies, that *our children may know to what source they may look for a remission of their sins"* (2 Nephi 25:26, emphasis added).

A MODERN EXAMPLE

Friends of ours struggled along in a flawed marriage. It wasn't a bad marriage. It just wasn't what they wanted. After ten years of marriage the husband launched an affair and left his covenants. He told his wife that there was no way to fix their marriage, so he was moving on.

He was right. There was no way he could fix the imperfections in his marriage with the tools he had been using. No way. This fact is enough to make a person desperate—which is exactly what is needed for us to be open to God. We must be desperate enough to throw ourselves on His mercy. "Wherefore, how great the importance to make these things known unto the inhabitants of the earth, that they may know that *there is no flesh that can dwell in the presence of God, save it be through the merits, and mercy, and grace of the Holy Messiah* . . . (2 Nephi 2:8, emphasis added).

Rather than depend on our own limited abilities, we can have the humility to go to God for help. And He is mighty to save—both souls and marriages. This is what the Book of Mormon calls faith unto repentance (see Alma 34:14-17). When we trust God enough to turn our lives over to Him, He does miracles.

FAITH UNTO REPENTENCE

Rather than turn his life over to God, our aforementioned friend continued to use his own bright mind to try to figure things out. But he always came up with the same dismal conclusions. He correctly judged that he just couldn't change his imperfect marriage, yet he failed to understand the true redeeming power of Christ—power over sin, mortal failings, and feelings of hopelessness. Faith unto repentance means that we trust Jesus enough to turn our lives over to Him. We give up governance of our lives and turn that over to God. We may pray, as Fosdick did, "Fill us with Thyself, that we may no longer be a burden to ourselves."[47]

Every serious relationship will get to the point of desperation. At some point we know our partner well enough to be irritated and to know that the sources of our irritation are not likely to disappear. That is the watershed moment. We can leave the relationship, smolder in sullen resentment, or repent. God recommends repentance.

Repentance "denotes a change of mind, i.e., a fresh view about God, about oneself, and about the world. Since we are born into conditions of mortality, repentance comes to mean a turning of the heart and will to God, and a renunciation of sin to which we are naturally inclined" (Bible Dictionary, p. 760).

Since the universal sin is pride,[48] the heart of repentance is giving up our self-sufficiency, our sense that we can set our own lives right. We must turn ourselves over to God. He can make sense of our fractured and flawed lives. We cannot.

Curing pride

President Ezra Taft Benson's great sermon on pride has the keys to our repentance.

> Pride is a sin that can readily be seen in others but is rarely admitted in our-selves. . . . Selfishness is one of the more common faces of pride. "How everything affects me" is the center of all that matters—self-conceit, self-pity, worldly self-fulfillment, self-gratification, and self-seeking.
>
> The antidote for pride is humility—meekness, submissiveness (see Alma 7:23). It is the broken heart and contrite spirit.
>
> God will have a humble people. Either we can choose to be humble or we can be compelled to be humble. . . . Let us choose to be humble.
>
> We can choose to humble ourselves by conquering enmity toward our brothers and sisters, esteeming them as ourselves, and lifting them as high or higher than we are.[49]

The irony of pride is that those who are most talented are those who are most vulnerable to this leprosy of the soul. The world may esteem great talent as a blessing, but it is nothing to God in the absence of humility. "Only when we change our hearts through personal repentance can the burdensome weight of sin really be lifted from our weary shoulders."[50]

The fix-it mind set

When I follow the natural man's method for marital change, I set out to tell my partner in fair, balanced ways what she is doing that irritates me. Then she can change herself based on my input, and we will both be happy.

Elder Joe J. Christensen taught us in General Conference about the problem with this approach:

> As a newlywed, Sister Lola Walters read in a magazine that in

order to strengthen a marriage a couple should have regular, candid sharing sessions in which they would list any mannerisms they found annoying. She wrote: "We were to name five things we found annoying, and I started off...I told him I didn't like the way he ate grapefruit. He peeled it and ate it like an orange! Nobody else I knew ate grapefruit like that. Could a girl be expected to spend a lifetime, even eternity, watching her husband eat grapefruit like an orange! After I finished, it was his turn to tell the things he disliked about me...He said, 'Well, to tell the truth, I can't think of anything I don't like about you, Honey.' Gasp. I quickly turned my back because I didn't know how to explain the tears that had filled my eyes and were running down my face..." Whenever I hear of married couples being incompatible, I always wonder if they are suffering from what I now call the Grapefruit Syndrome.[51]

As Marleen S. Williams observes, "each [spouse] believes the other is the cause of the dispute and that convincing the spouse of his or her guilt will then solve the problem."[52] The problem is that when we are accused, we dig in our heels. When we approach our partners as spousal renewal projects, they are likely to respond in kind. We get caught up in an endless and hopeless tangle of accusation and recrimination.

In fact, any time we feel irritated with our spouses, that irritation is not an invitation to call our spouses to repentance but an invitation to call ourselves to repent. We are irritated because of our own lack of faith and humility.

In contrast, when we have the "mind of Christ," we see our spouses in a new way. We, like Jesus, look upon the injured, erring, and downtrodden—the whole human race—with compassion. The Prophet Joseph Smith challenged us: "The nearer we get to our heavenly Father, the more we are disposed to look with compassion on perishing [spouses]; we feel that we want to take them upon our shoulders, and cast their sins behind our backs. . . . if you would have God have mercy on you, have mercy on [your spouses]."[53]

We can see our spouses with compassion rather than with irritation.

Flat tires in our relationship

Appreciating is more powerful than correcting. Appreciation inflates the tires on which we travel. Criticism is a slow leak in those tires.

Marital dialogue in the movie "Accidental Tourist" brilliantly illustrates the problem. None of us wants to be seen as a problem to be fixed.

Sarah: "You know, Macon, the trouble with you is..."

Macon: "Sarah, look, don't even start. If that doesn't sum up everything that's wrong with being married: 'Macon, the trouble with you is...I know you better than you know yourself, Macon.'"

Sarah: "The trouble with you is you don't believe in people opening up. You think everyone should stay in their own little sealed package."

Macon: "Okay. Let's say that that's true. Let's say for now that you do know what the trouble with me is . . . and that the reason I don't want to hear about this specific thing is that I can't open up; if we agree on all that, can we drop it?!"

President Hinckley describes this miserable cycle of correction and paybacks in strong terms: "Is there anything more weak or beggarly than the disposition to wear out one's life in an unending round of bitter thoughts and scheming gestures toward those who may have affronted us?"[54]

This is a fitting place to recall that God commands us to repent ourselves and to love others–especially our spouses: "Thou shalt love thy wife with all thy heart, and shalt cleave unto her and none else" (D&C 42:22).

The key to repentance

When we study those in the scriptures who were most dramatically or powerfully changed by repentance, we find an interesting commonality in their mantra.

Alma the Younger Alma 36:18	Publican Luke 18:13	King Benjamin's people Mosiah 4:2	Brother of Jared Ether 3:3
O Jesus, thou Son of God, have mercy on me,	*God be merciful to me, a sinner.*	*O have mercy, and apply the atoning blood of Christ.*	*Thou hast been merciful unto us. O Lord, look upon me in pity.*

The scriptures are replete with those who called on God for mercy. In fact, the context for Amulek's directive to pray in all times and places is "to call upon his holy name, that *he would have mercy upon you; Yea, cry unto him for mercy;* for he is mighty to save" (Alma 34:17-18, emphasis added). A whole-souled acknowledgment of our dependence on God is a very good working definition of humility. This is where the miracles begin. This is where despair is replaced with growth.

When we humbly turn our minds, our lives, and our purposes over to God, He will refine us. We begin to see with new eyes. We feel with new warmth and goodness. We gladly give our time and energy to bless those around us—especially those with whom we have made covenants.

Two processes were named above for dealing with our natural human narrow-mindedness: getting heaven's perspective and being open to our partner's point of view. This chapter deals with humility and repentance as keys that unlock heaven's perspective. Humility and repentance also open us up to our partner's perspective. That will be discussed more in Chapter 7 on charity.

WHAT REPENTANCE DOES AND DOESN'T LOOK LIKE

I have a good friend who has a keen mind and was trained as a professional. In midlife he set up a business to practice his profession. But the business failed. He took part-time work as a custodian. The disappointment and humiliation were painful to him. He became increasingly irritable and gloomy. His health declined and his marriage suffered.

We talked regularly. I thought I saw a trend over time. For a while he talked about a few challenges he and his wife faced as they tried to manage their large family and their small income. Over time these concerns and irritations grew into judgments. He began describing his wife as selfish. He provided an example of her selfishness. The wife complained about the damage his little dog did to the crowded house. He bristled that she didn't care about his canine companion. (But he didn't work with his wife to address her concerns.)

Over time, his complaint grew more global. "I think she may be the most selfish person I know." Yet that was not the end. Satan is not content until he has fully re-written our history removing every ember of warmth and goodness. "I don't think I ever loved her," he said.

My heart ached. He had thrown away decades of heavenly blessings because of his current unhappiness. He had re-written history with wifely disappointment as its theme. Satan had robbed him of past, present, and future. At the center of Satan's mischief was pride—that enmity that makes us enemies to each other.

Brother Kent Brooks condemns not only the way we use weapons of war against each other, but that we also keep studying and magnifying each other's offences. "To bury our weapons of war yet continue to rebroadcast a 'wide-screen' version of old battles and old wounds, complete with 'instant replay,' 'slow-motion,' and our own exaggerated form of 'special effects,' undermines the process of healing and the prospects for growth—for both spouses."[55]

Many of us grew up dreading humility and repentance. They felt like an unhappy encounter with humiliation. But, as we mature spiritually, we come to recognize humility and repentance as heavenly blessings. We cast off the tattered ways of the natural man and put on the robe of righteousness. It is sweet.

It is true, as Elder Neal A. Maxwell has observed, that "the enlarging of the soul requires not only some remodeling, but some excavating. Hypocrisy, guile, and other imbedded traits do not go gladly or easily."[56] Yet that excavating is not painful when we see the glorious purposes behind it.

The whole script of the husband and his "selfish" wife could have been rewritten with a very different journey and outcome if God had been given the stylus. The husband could have humbly turned much of his pain over to God. The wife could have rallied support and compassion for her burdened husband. And both could have drawn on the tradition of growth, goodness, and faithfulness that filled their earlier marital history.

USING REPENTANCE TO CHANGE OUR MARRIAGES

How do we use repentance to make our marriages stronger? The first step is the humility to know that our perceptions are very limited. We rarely know our partner's heart or God's purposes.

Then we learn to call on God. Every day. Every hour. We cry out with all great repenters: "O Jesus, thou Son of God, have mercy on my fallen and troubled soul. Fill me with Thee. Soften my heart. Give me healing peace." There is power in submission. As Paul astutely observed, "Therefore I take pleasure in infirmities, in reproaches, in necessities, in persecutions, in distresses for Christ's sake: for *when* I am weak, then am I strong" (2 Corinthians. 12:10, emphasis added).

Very often our self-sufficiency gets in God's way. In the spirit of humility, we listen to our partner and we listen to God. We replace despair with an enlarged openness to Christ-like goodness.

EXAMPLES OF REPENTANCE

Let me provide some simple examples. For reasons that I cannot explain, I like kitchen counters to be tidy and free of clutter. (Oddly, this strong preference does not seem to apply to my desk and my other work areas.) For years I wondered why Nancy occasionally sinned in this area. Why did such a decent person leave things on the kitchen counters?

After years of simmering irritation, it finally occurred to me that this was not Nancy's problem. It was my problem. If something on the counter is bothering me, I can put it away. I can wipe away crumbs.

That is repentance, glorious repentance. It is very liberating.

There are other examples. Nancy is the kindest, gentlest, and most considerate human being I have ever known. I love being with her! But there is a price to be paid for Nancy's kindness. She is not especially decisive. When I am hungry or in a hurry I can work up a very good case of irritation when she vacillates while the restaurant server waits. I can get quite angry when she changes her mind about something we have discussed and jointly decided.

Or I can repent. And there are many dimensions to repentance—including the willingness to set my partner up for success. For example, I can help Nancy think through the restaurant options. "You have always liked chicken salad." She and I can even discuss her food mood on the way to the restaurant.

We can also make allowances for our partners. I can allow Nancy a little more time for making decisions. I can expect some wavering. (As tightly wound as I am, this is a real sacrifice. And this is just as it should be. I cannot truly repent without sacrificing some of the natural man!)

I observed another interesting opportunity for repentance in a capable couple we knew in Alabama. The wife loved ice cream. Every once in a while she would have a scoop or two. For her it was a special treat. Her husband apparently had ambitions for her slimness. Any time she thought about ice cream, he tried to talk her out of it. Every time she ate ice cream, he grimaced like a man in pain.

I feel quite certain that if he gave up his effort to regulate his wife's ice cream consumption, she would regulate it much better than his brow-beatings were regulating it. He could repent of his effort to micromanage his wife. He could appreciate her natural beauty. He could love her and let her be in charge of her ice cream decisions.

The media provide a very specific image of the perfect man and woman. Our culture would have us obsess about perfect proportions, firm muscles, and flawless skin. But plastic surgery and relentless exercise are not the answer. Charity is. We can repent of our narrow, trivial, superficial demands. We can recognize that a person is beautiful because we choose to love her or him—and not because the luck of genetics compels our love.

I love Irving Becker's observation: "If you don't like someone, the way he holds his spoon will make you furious; if you do like him, he can turn his plate over into your lap and you won't mind."[57]

Love is not a happy accident; It is a choice.

THE BLESSING OF IRRITATION

Irritation can be our friend. It alerts us to the risk of blisters when we sense a pebble in our shoes. In marriage, irritation serves the vital function of alerting us that something we are doing (or feeling, or saying) is creating a sore.

While the natural man is inclined to think that the problem is our partner, the man of Christ knows that the irritation is probably the result of some faulty thinking—some troublesome assumption and expectation nested in our unconscious. We can remove the judging even if we cannot track down the troublesome assumptions.

Some years ago God taught me an ironic truth. I don't have the right to correct anyone I don't love. You see the irony! I am inclined to correct my partner when I don't feel loving. When I *do* feel loving, irritations roll off my soul like water on a duck's back.

That is not to say that I should never make my wishes known to my wife. We certainly have the right to express preferences and make requests. It would be foolish to leave my partner in the dark about my preferences. "Honey I enjoy your other soups more than the celery soup. Which are your favorites?"

But expressing preferences is not the same as dwelling on irritations and cultivating grievances. I should use irritation as an invitation for me to repent. "Behold, this is not my doctrine, to stir up the hearts of men with anger, one against another; but this is my doctrine, that such things should be done away" (3 Nephi 11:30).

There is a popular quote attributed to J. Golden Kimball: "I'll never go to hell. I repent too damn fast." Whatever the merits of the expression, the sentiment is right. Any irritation can prompt us to immediate humility and immediate repentance. We do not have to let irritations accumulate and form ruthless gangs that will savage our love.

For those evil judgments that will not go easily, we can invoke the prayer of all repenters, "O Jesus, Thou Son of God, have mercy on me and my poor, narrow soul. Fill me with Thy graciousness." This is the way to cast out evil spirits in our souls.

I think the statement posted in front of a country church in Arkansas is true: "A happy marriage is the union of two forgivers."[58]

POSTSCRIPT

If, as you read this chapter, you found yourself thinking how much your partner needs it, I encourage you to re-read the chapter with yourself in mind.

CREATING YOUR OWN STORY

Thoughts

Think of a time when you have turned irritation into a blessing by repenting of judgments and assumptions. How did you do it? How can you make that a more regular part of your relationship?

Feelings

Will you institutionalize the plea of repenters ("Oh, God, have mercy on me, a sinner!") in your life in order to draw more heavenly goodness into your life? Note that Amulek's invitation to pray in our fields houses, closets, secret places, and wilderness are all prefaced with "cry unto him for mercy for he is mighty to save" (Alma 34:18). Cry for mercy in your marriage. Offer God the broken heart that opens Heaven's gates.

Actions

Rather than be bothered by the things we want to change in our partners and marriages, we can learn to accept humanness and flaws in our partners. We can laugh at the foibles that bedevil all of us. We can pray for mercy for ourselves and our partners. Because each of us desperately needs mercy, we can offer mercy to each other.

NOTES

43   Roy Baumeister, *Meanings of Life*, New York: Guilford Press [1991], 113-14.

44   Jonathan Haidt, *The Happiness Hypothesis: Finding Modern Truth in Ancient Wisdom*, New York: Basic Books [2006], 71.

45   Douglas E. Brinley and D. K. Judd (Eds.), *Living in a Covenant Marriage*, Salt Lake City: Deseret Book [2004], 121.

46   See Andrew Christensen and Neil S. Jacobson, *Reconcilable Differences*, New York: Guilford Press [2000].

47   *The Meaning of Faith*, New York: Association Press [1918], 213.

48   See Ezra Taft Benson, "Beware of Pride," *Ensign*, May 1989, 4.

49   *Ensign*, May 1989, 4.

50   *Covenant Marriage*, 94-95.

51   *Ensign*, May 1995, 64-66.

52   *Covenant Marriage*, 84.

53   *Teachings of the Prophet Joseph Smith*, 241.

54   Gordon B. Hinckley, "Of You It Is Required to Forgive," *Ensign*, June 1991, 4.

55   *Covenant Marriage*, 111.

56   "Endure it Well," *Ensign*, May 1990, 33.

57   *Reader's Digest, Pocket Treasury of Great Quotations* [1975], 19.

58   Batesville, AR church, Aug. 25, 2003.

CHAPTER FIVE

PURITY:

"How then can I do this great wickedness,
and sin against God?"

We live in a time of great moral pollution. Even if we individually take moral purity seriously, we are surrounded by media and culture that celebrate sex as the currency of the realm. Immodesty commands our attention. Lust encourages our warped thinking. Our screen heroes and our real-life national heroes are as casual about sex as about a night on the town. Our contemporary attitude toward sex creates a desolating scourge.

President Kimball has warned us that "infidelity is one of the great sins of our generation. The movies, the books, the magazine stories all seem to glamorize the faithlessness of husbands and wives. To the world nothing is holy, not even marriage vows . . . It reminds us of Isaiah, who said: 'Woe unto them that call evil good, and good evil. . . .' (Isaiah 5:20)."[59]

AN ANCIENT ENCOUNTER

One of the great examples of moral ascendance was Joseph of Israel. His encounter with Potiphar's wife is told in just six verses in the book of Genesis.

And it came to pass after these things, that his master's wife cast her eyes upon Joseph; and she said, Lie with me.

But he refused, and said unto his master's wife, Behold, my master wotteth not what is with me in the house, and he hath committed all that he hath to my hand;

There is none greater in this house than I; neither hath he kept back any thing from me but thee, because thou art his wife: *how then can I do this great wickedness, and sin against God?*

And it came to pass, as she spake to Joseph day by day, that he hearkened not unto her, to lie by her, or to be with her.

And it came to pass about this time, that Joseph went into the house to do his business; and there was none of the men of the house there within.

And she caught him by his garment, saying, Lie with me: and he left his garment in her hand, and fled, and got him out (Gen. 39:7-12, emphasis added).

We honor Joseph's valiance and purity. He was far from his home ward with its attendant accountability. Potiphar's wife was alluring and powerful. Yet he resisted her without hesitation. What an example!

AN ENRICHED ACCOUNT

The Book of Jasher contains an account of the encounters between Joseph and Potiphar's wife that is much richer and more detailed than that in the Old Testament. Whether the book that circulates today as the Book of Jasher is the same book as that referred to in Joshua and 2 Samuel is uncertain. John Taylor recommended that the book we know as the Book of Jasher be considered as history but not as revelation. Whether the Jasher account of Joseph is perfectly historical, it is perfectly instructive. It is as dramatic as anything that has ever come from Hollywood, while being morally inspiring.

Since the account of Potiphar's wife enticing Joseph consumes over

3,000 words in the Book of Jasher, I will re-tell the story in summary form. When I go beyond summarizing the story as it appears in the Book of Jasher, I put my comments in brackets.

Potiphar brought Joseph to manage his holdings. God prospered all that Joseph touched. Joseph had "beautiful eyes and [a] comely appearance" unlike any in the land of Egypt. Potiphar's wife, Zelicah, found herself drawn to him. "She coveted his beauty in her heart, and her soul was fixed upon Joseph, and she enticed him day after day, and Zelicah persuaded Joseph daily, but Joseph did not lift up his eyes to behold his master's wife" (v.16). [Joseph was exemplary. He did not even look at Zelicah!]

Zelicah flattered Joseph telling him that she had never seen such a beautiful slave. Joseph responded that the One who created him created all mankind. She replied that his eyes dazzled all the inhabitants of Egypt. He observed that when he died his eyes would frighten her. She praised him for his words. He replied that his words were beautiful when he praised God. When she praised his hair, he begged her to stop and take care of her business. Joseph was not to be won with flattery [which is one of Satan's favorite tools for luring us into affairs].

Zelicah persisted. "She enticed him daily with her discourse to lie with her, or even to look at her, but Joseph would not hearken to her" (v.23). So she threatened him with bondage and death. Joseph's reply was noble: "Surely God who created man looseth the fetters of prisoners, and it is he who will deliver me from thy prison and from thy judgment" (v. 25).

When she was unable to seduce Joseph, Zelicah fell into a depression. When her friends came to visit her they could not imagine that such a wealthy woman could be unhappy. So she made a banquet for them. She gave them fruit to cut and peel and had Joseph appear before them. "And they all cut their hands with the knives that they had in their hands, and all the citrons that were in their hands were filled with blood" (v. 29). [Hollywood never scripted a more dramatic scene!] They could not look away from Joseph.

Zelicah challenged them. If you cut yourselves after looking at

Joseph, how can I manage myself when he is constantly in my house? How can I keep from perishing? [Satan has inspired the lustful question: How can you possibly live around such a magnificent man without having sex?]

Zelicah's misery increased. Her friends encouraged her to seduce him by any means necessary. So she attacked him. But he broke from her and ran away.

Later she asked Joseph how he could make her suffer so. She insisted that he would be the death of her. [It seems that she had turned to using guilt on him: Joseph was responsible for her misery!] Joseph replied that he would not dishonor his master. "How then canst thou speak these words unto me, and how can I do this great evil and sin to God and to thy husband?" (v. 45) [This sentence is reminiscent of Joseph's words in the Genesis account.]

She ignored his counsel and continued daily to entice him. Then a holiday came. As all the people left for the festivities, she made excuses and remained in the house. She dressed herself in her most exotic clothes, put on her finest jewelry, and applied the finest makeup and perfume. Then she took up a place where she knew Joseph would pass. But as soon as he saw her, he turned away. She begged him to stay and continue his work.

As he sat to do his work, she stood before him. In desperation she threatened him. "As the king liveth if thou wilt not perform my request thou shalt die this day, and she hastened and stretched forth her other hand and drew a sword from beneath her garments, and she placed it upon Joseph's neck, and she said, Rise and perform my request, and if not thou diest this day" (v. 53). [Many weaker souls would have justified submitting to her threats. Not Joseph!]

When Joseph fled, she grabbed his robe and pulled it from him as he departed. When her seduction has failed, she changed into her regular clothes. She sent a messenger to gather the people of the household, then made her accusation: "See what a Hebrew your master has brought to me in the house, for he came this day to lie with me" (v. 57).

Everyone was indignant with Joseph. Potiphar was enraged. Joseph was punished with severe stripes—even though Joseph proclaimed his innocence and wise men recognized the inconsistencies in Zelicah's story. Joseph was stuck in the prison house for 12 years! [A lesser man would have cursed God for punishing him for his virtue!]

Incredibly, Zelicah visited him in prison for three months trying to persuade him to submit to her in exchange for his freedom. Even in such desperate circumstances, Joseph would have none of it. "It is better for me to remain in this house than to hearken to thy words, to sin against God (v. 78, Book of Jasher, Chapter XLIV).

While Hollywood makes drama out of lust and seduction, the truly great dramas celebrate something different: faithfulness and holiness. Much like Jesus, Joseph "suffered temptations but gave no heed unto them" (D&C 20:22). In a time when lust is the backdrop to almost all relationships, Joseph stands as an example to us of a pure heart. Joseph honored his covenants above pleasure, lust, threats, prison, or convenience. He gave no place for evil.

MODERN SUBTLETY

Today Satan attacks us with subtle and indirect means. He gets us inappropriately close to someone who is not our spouse under the guise of missionary work, friendship, or helpfulness. He subtly builds inappropriate emotional bonds while quieting our consciences with weak rationalizations. Perhaps this is Satan's favorite ploy with those who desire goodness and are filled with compassion. The Book of Mormon describes his strategy: "And others will he pacify, and lull them away into carnal security, that they will say: All is well in Zion; yea, Zion prospereth, all is well—and thus the devil cheateth their souls, and leadeth them away carefully down to hell" (2 Nephi 28:21).

AN UNCHANGING STANDARD

Ancient Joseph of Israel may be especially instructive to us. While he was raised with righteous standards, his experience in Egypt was similar in many ways to the seduction and evil we experience in our culture. Just as Zelicah relentlessly lured him toward evil, so our common talk, T.V. and movies suggest that chastity is outmoded.

Modern prophets have unapologetically declared the same standard that Joseph lived by.

> There are those married people who permit their eyes to wander and their hearts to become vagrant, who think it is not improper to flirt a little, to share their hearts and have desire for someone other then the wife or the husband. The Lord says in no uncertain terms: 'Thou shalt love thy wife with all thy heart, and shalt cleave unto her and none else' (D&C 42:22).
>
> And, when the Lord says *all* thy heart, it allows for no sharing nor dividing nor depriving. . . . The words *none else* eliminate everyone and everything. The spouse then becomes preeminent in the life of the husband or wife, and neither social life nor occupational life nor political life nor any other interest nor person nor thing shall ever take precedence over the companion spouse. . . .
>
> Marriage presupposes total allegiance and total fidelity. Each spouse takes the partner with the understanding that he or she gives totally to the spouse all the heart, strength, loyalty, honor, and affection, with all dignity. Any divergence is sin; any sharing of the heart is transgression. As we should have "an eye single to the glory of God," so should we have an eye, an ear, a heart single to the marriage and the spouse and family.[60]

AN EXAMPLE OF DECEPTION

A good friend taught me a lot about the subtle process that Satan uses. She is an earnest, married Latter-day Saint. She caught me at a social gathering to tell me of a great friendship she had developed with a man in her ward. She and he enjoyed great discussions about the gospel. Sometimes he called her from work. Occasionally they met downtown for lunch. He bought her little gifts. She told me how much she enjoyed her companionship with the man. I was worried. Then she told me how good the man was with children . . . and how she wished her husband would be as sensitive. Then I knew.

The devil had carefully woven her discontent about her husband together with her affection for another man. The effect was devastating to her marriage. She was trying to find some way to leave her husband while still doing all she believed was right. It is a damned-if-you-do and damned-if-you-don't situation. She does not enjoy her marriage and family. Yet she can't find any way to have what she thinks she wants. She is trapped. She is right where the devil wants her. She is miserable.

The devil's methods for tricking us are predictable. Trouble starts with behaviors that seem very innocent. We do good, helpful things: supporting a troubled neighbor, sharing gospel ideas with a ward member, working closely with another person on a ward activity, listening to the troubles of a co-worker. All of these kindnesses are good. But the trouble begins as a person starts to feel responsible or very close to someone who is not his or her marriage partner. An affection is growing that claims part of the heart that belongs only to the spouse.

The covenant we make with God to avoid all sexual relations outside of marriage precludes not only physical, but also romantic relationships outside of marriage, even if they are only mental or emotional.

In his talk, "The Eternal Nature of the Law of Chastity," Elder Gene R. Cook has said that we do not have the right to stimulate or be stimulated by anyone who is not our spouse. That is a high standard! We do not have the right to allow or entertain sexual feelings for anyone but our spouses. In the early stages of extramarital flirting, the intoxicating feeling of someone's affection and the sense of our innocence may blind us to the seriousness of our situation.

STAGES OF UNFAITHFULNESS

The unfaithfulness moves to a more serious and dangerous stage of unfaithfulness when one or both of the people declare their relationship "special." They would never dream of "doing anything immoral or improper." But a person increasingly makes excuses to see the special friend. They plan their schedules to assure that they will be together. Cards, notes and gifts are exchanged.

One tell-tale indicator that a relationship has moved to a dangerous stage is worrying about what people may say about the time or affection that you are sharing with the other person. Another indicator is making excuses or telling lies to hide the time or resources spent on the other person. This is the point at which "friends" begin sharing more of their daily thoughts and feelings with each other than with their spouses. At this point the spouse is displaced as the key recipient of heartfelt communication as emotional intimacy is given to an outsider. These are sure signs that you are doing something wrong.

At this stage, sacred covenants have already been violated and permanent damage lurks. The rightful place of spouse in a person's heart is crowded by affections for another person. At this stage of unfaithfulness the person is especially likely to be finding fault with his or her spouse. The spouse is compared to the special friend: "I wish my husband were as good with children as Fred." "I wish my wife were as alert and interesting as Mandy."

At this stage a person is misled enough to start weaving fantastic fantasies. One form of the fantasizing may sound like "Maybe the Lord wants me to be happy with this other person—and in my case divorce would be sanctioned by Him." In a more malignant form, it may sound like: "Maybe the Lord will take my husband so that John and I can be together. Somehow, someday, the Lord will work this beautiful relationship out for us."

Ouch! The Lord does not want us to drop out of His finishing school at the first sign of challenge. Also, the Lord is not a heavenly hit man who takes out selected children in order to satisfy our whims and lustful fantasies. He asks instead that we learn to love each other and overlook the inevitable faults we discover. He asks that we honor commitments and strengthen our partners. He asks that we be as good and kind to our partners as we would have them be to us. This is the Christian mandate in its most soul-stretching form.

This stage of unfaithfulness can be a full-blown addiction even if physical intimacies have not been shared. The treatment for it can be wrenching. But rationalizing that it is not a problem and that we can handle it may only delay the pain and increase the risk of further, permanent damage to the family.

The final stage of unfaithfulness begins officially with the showing of any physical affection. It is easy for "special friends" to justify a squeeze. Even a kiss seems innocent enough. The "friends" may be determined to avoid immorality at all costs. They may think that full sexual expression is not even to be considered. But intoxication with the pleasures of romance make the insistent and powerful pleading of biological urges more and more difficult to ignore. Even if a couple exercises the restraint to avoid having intercourse, the damage to family relations that comes from divided loyalties and ugly dishonesty is terrific and tragic. Trust is destroyed. Covenants, with all of their glorious promises, are wasted.

But it does not have to be that way. At any point in the process we can repent. The more time and emotion that we have invested in our fantasy, the harder it is to repent. Satan will not let go of us gladly.

We may try to kid ourselves into thinking that we can somehow honor our covenants while holding a special place in our heart for the "soul mate." But we lie to ourselves and to God in believing this. We violate our covenants. The devil must roar with laughter as he observes us feeling confined by our sacred covenants while yearning for something that does not and cannot satisfy. Wickedness never was–and never will be–happiness (Alma 41:10).

An ounce of prevention

Latter-day Saints should be alert to the predictable temptations that Satan uses to break up marriages. We should monitor our behavior and our feelings closely. By being alert to the danger signs we can prevent the problems that begin so innocently but end so disastrously.

There are several guidelines that can help prevent trouble.

1. Do not allow the seeds of lust to germinate. Do not look on another

woman or man with lust. Do not entertain mental fantasies of romance or passion. Do not let your mind be poisoned with the sick encounters in soap operas, worldly literature, or any form of pornography.

2. Never make excuses to spend time alone with a person of the opposite sex who is not your spouse. Guard the level of emotional intimacy you build with a non-spouse. As Shirley Glass, a scholar on faithfulness, said, we should maintain a wall between us and those who are not friends to our marriage—who threaten it in any way. We may open a window to those who are friends of our marriage. And there should be no walls nor windows between us and our spouses. We should be as one.

3. Take responsibility for the messages that you give. You do not have the right to be "cute" or flirty with anyone but your spouse. Do not use cards, gifts or charm to win the affection of anyone who is not your spouse.

4. Do not allow your heart to dwell on anyone. Push daydreaming of any person but your spouse out of your mind promptly. When you are worried about the intruder, pray for him or her and trust Heavenly Father to care for him or her. The untangling of excuses and emotional dependence can be the hardest part of overcoming the addiction.

5. If you find yourself making excuses for continuing the relationship, you are addicted. Get help. Talk with your bishop or stake president. Seek out the help of friends who will help you overcome your addiction.

6. Spend more enjoyable time with your spouse. Have weekly dates doing those things that you enjoy together. Find ways to improve your relationship. Be patient. Recognize that many of our frustrations with our spouses are built on the false assumption that they ought to be a certain way. Change your assumptions. Recognize that even the best marriages have more and less satisfying times. Be patient. Be true to your covenants. Enjoy your partner as he or she is. It is easy to believe that things will never be right with your spouse. Trust the Lord that He can heal all wounds.

7. Renew your spiritual efforts. Turn to the Lord in prayer. Ask for strength to put temptation out of your mind. Fill your empty places

with service, scripture study, and love for your family.

8. Don't set yourself up for failure. Don't allow yourself to spend time alone with the person. Avoiding is better than resisting. Make your spouse a partner in all of your efforts to help a person of the opposite sex.

9. Keep your soul free of the soul-numbing barrenness of pornography. The greatest sin of pornography may be that it reduces the sacrament of intimacy to a random and wanton act of self-gratification. Preserve or renew your awe in the blessing of simple acts of affection.

10. Celebrate the sweet gift of companionship. The amazing message from our marriage partners is: "I'm trusting you with my life, my body, my hopes, my dreams. Please be kind and gentle." Each of us should rejoice in the sacred gift of spousal trust. If we have squandered any part of it, we should work to re-qualify for it.

As my wise colleague James Marshall observes, "The grass is greener on the side of the fence you water." If we tend our own little patch, even with all its weeds and rocks, we will find a joy that passes understanding. If we sit on the fence and dream, we will lose even our allotted garden spot. And the devil knows that.

We should be prepared for Satan's attacks. He offers love, fun and a satisfying life. But it is a lie. He wants to get us to violate our covenants. But he has no joy to deliver on his grandiose promises. He is the master of misery. That is all he has to offer.

If we have been unwise enough to have been caught in a trap, we may repent. When we honor covenants made with our Heavenly Father we are always blessed. Always. Sometimes Father's process requires us to be patient. Sometimes He requires us to bear discomfort. But He always blesses those who obey eternal laws. And the blessings are in incredible disproportion to the price we have paid.

"To those who claim their love is dead, let them return home with all their loyalty, fidelity, honor, and cleanness, and the love that has become but embers will flare up with scintillating flame again. If love wanes or dies, it is often infidelity of thought or act that gave the lethal potion."[61]

The joy of fidelity

Fidelity may seem to be confining. It always will—unless we adopt God's perspective. "Through the lens of spirituality we see all the commandments of God as invitations to blessings. Obedience and sacrifice, loyalty and love, fidelity and family, all appear in eternal perspective."[62]

Those who have loved faithfully and patiently reap a harvest of joy and companionship. This sweet truth is acknowledged even by secular scholars: "For true lovers at all points in history, a fleeting touch on the cheek from the one they adore will be worth more than six hours in 37 positions with someone they do not."[63]

Those who resist the lure and guile of Satan, those who honor covenants, those who tend the little garden of their own covenants, will enjoy sweetness in this life and rewards unmeasured in the world to come.

As usual, Satan's lies are extravagant—but empty. In contrast God's promises are sure. When we, like Joseph, quietly honor our covenants—even making sacrifices and fighting temptation—God will reward us with blessings unfathomable to those who have grabbed pleasure over principle: "Be glad in the LORD, and rejoice, ye righteous: and shout for joy, all ye that are upright in heart" (Psalms 32:11). "Give, and it shall be given unto you; good measure, pressed down, and shaken together, and running over, shall men give into your bosom. For with the same measure that ye mete withal it shall be measured to you again" (Luke 6:38).

Postcript

Please note that the book in the reading list by Glass and Staeheli is especially focused on helping couples recover from affairs.

Creating Your Own Story

Thoughts

Do you notice times when you feel drawn toward someone who is not your spouse? Have you purified your heart so that you choose obedience over the ego-buzz of romance? Do you push away temptation and call on Heaven for mercy?

Feelings

Are you cultivating appreciation for sweet companionship in your marriage? Are you consciously grateful for the blessing of simple affection with your spouse?

Actions

Have you set a standard for yourself to avoid spending time alone with a person of the opposite sex?

Have you carefully monitored your words and actions to be sure that you do not flirt with anyone but your spouse? What might you do differently to be more clear in your commitment to your marriage?

Do you carefully keep yourself out of situations where flirting and immorality are common or acceptable?

Do you avoid websites, movies, and entertainment that turn intimacy into a matter of lust?

Do you share your appreciation for your spouse with friends so that they know of your commitment and affection for her or him?

NOTES

59 Spencer W. Kimball, *The Miracle of Forgiveness*, Salt Lake City: Bookcraft [1969], 250.

60 Spencer W. Kimball, *Faith Precedes the Miracle*, Salt Lake City: Deseret Book [1973], 141-43.

61 *Faith Precedes the Miracle*, 147.

62 Dallin H. Oaks, *Pure in Heart*, Salt Lake City: Bookcraft [1988], 123.

63 Desmond Morris, *Intimate Behavior*, New York: Random House [1971], 85.

CHAPTER SIX

CONSECRATION:

"Zion cannot be built up unless it is by the principles of the law of the celestial kingdom."

Living the law of consecration moves us from gospel hobbyists to career disciples. It is a mark of true followers. President Benson taught us about this law:

> "We covenant to live the law of consecration. This law is that we consecrate our time, talents, strength, property, and money for the upbuilding of the kingdom of God on this earth and the establishment of Zion.

> Until one abides by the laws of obedience, sacrifice, the gospel, and chastity, he cannot abide the law of consecration, which is the law pertaining to the celestial kingdom. "Zion cannot be built up unless it is by the principles of the law of the celestial kingdom" (D&C 105:5). The law of consecration is a celestial law, not an economic experiment.[64]

The law of consecration is foreign to the natural man. To such it appears as a way for the church to get rich and exercise control over us.

Those who know God and have experimented with His ways know otherwise. They know that the more they turn their lives over to God, the better their lives become. The ultimate joy is to surrender completely to God. We turn everything over to Him and life gets inexpressibly good.

Elder Maxwell underscores this irony: "Consecration is the only surrender which is also a victory. It brings release from the raucous, overpopulated cell block of selfishness and emancipation from the dark prison of pride."[65]

Various metaphors might be used for consecration. Only the vines connected to the roots will bear fruit. Only that part of the car driven into the carwash can be cleaned. Only those train cars hooked to the engine can be pulled up the mountain. Only that which we bring to the altar can be sanctified and perfected.

To offer everything to God requires great faith. Joseph Smith said

For a man to lay down his all, his character and reputation, his honor and applause, his good name among men, his houses, his lands, his brothers and sisters, his wife and children, and even his own life also—counting all things but filth and dross for the excellency of the knowledge of Jesus Christ—requires more than mere belief or supposition that he is doing the will of God; but actual knowledge, realizing that, when these sufferings are ended he will enter into eternal rest, and be a partaker of the glory of God. *A religion that does not require the sacrifice of all things never has power sufficient to produce the faith necessary unto life and salvation;* for, from the first existence of man, the faith necessary unto the enjoyment of life and salvation never could be obtained without the sacrifice of all earthly things. It was through this sacrifice, and this only, that God has ordained that men should enjoy eternal life.[66]

While many of us tentatively experiment with trusting God, He waits patiently. He will answer every experiment with the same result: love, joy and peace are the fruits of trusting Him.

An ancient model of consecration

As a young man, Abraham was deeply troubled when his fathers "turned from their righteousness, and from the holy commandments which the Lord their God had given unto them, unto the worshiping of the gods of the heathen [and] utterly refused to hearken to my voice; For their hearts were set to do evil . . . (Abraham 1:5-6). The people were so totally devoid of light that they turned to sacrificing their own children. They sacrificed virgins and even attempted to slay Abraham. Nevertheless, over the years Abraham grew in faith and heavenly power.

Abraham was 100 years old when he and Sarah had the yearned-for son, Isaac. How they must have cherished their boy! How they must have rejoiced that their lives had been crowned with Isaac's miraculous birth!

According to tradition, Isaac was 30 years old when Abraham received the commandment to sacrifice his son. Imagine the soul-stretching pain of being asked to participate in a ritual he loathed, and to lose his cherished son!

The story is both poignant and instructive. There are rich details in the Book of Jasher account that may or may not be fully doctrinal but again are fully instructive. As with the story of Joseph, my own comments appear in brackets.

> At that time the word of the Lord came to Abraham, and he said unto him, Abraham, and he said, Here I am. [These words are wonderfully akin to those uttered by Jehovah in answer to His call to rescue the human race!]

> And he said to him, Take now thy son, thine only son whom thou lovest, even Isaac, and go to the land of Moriah, and offer him there for a burnt offering upon one of the mountains which shall be shown to thee, for there wilt thou see a cloud and the glory of the Lord. . . .

> And Abraham went with Isaac his son to bring him up as an offering before the Lord, as He had commanded him. . . .

> And whilst Abraham was proceeding with his son Isaac along the road, Satan came and appeared to Abraham in the figure of a very aged man, humble and of contrite spirit, and he approached Abraham and said to him, Art thou silly or brutish, that thou goest to do this thing this day to thine only son? . . .[There are always those

who will call our offerings to the Lord silly, pointless, and unnecessary!]

And Abraham rebuked him and said unto him, The Lord rebuke thee, O Satan, begone from us for we go by the commands of God.

And Satan was terrified at the voice of Abraham, and he went away from them, and the place again became dry land as it was at first.

And Abraham went with Isaac toward the place that God had told him. . . .

And Abraham took wood for a burnt offering and placed it upon his son Isaac, and he took the fire and the knife, and they both went to that place.

And when they were going along Isaac said to his father, Behold, I see here the fire and wood, and where then is the lamb that is to be the burnt offering before the Lord?

And Abraham answered his son Isaac, saying, The Lord has made choice of thee my son, to be a perfect burnt offering instead of the lamb (Chapter XXIII: 1-2, 20, 25, 38-40, 49-51).

Can we imagine Isaac's shock! "God wants you to be the burnt offering." How would you react? Many of us would suspect our fathers of being unhinged. But Isaac responded with magnificent grace. Even when his father probed his resolve, he was unflinching.

And Isaac said unto his father, *I will do all that the Lord spoke to thee with joy and cheerfulness of heart.*

And Abraham again said unto Isaac his son, Is there in thy heart any thought or counsel concerning this, which is not proper? tell me my son, I pray thee, O my son conceal it not from me.

And Isaac answered his father Abraham and said unto him, *O my father, as the Lord liveth and as thy soul liveth, there is nothing in my heart to cause me to deviate either to the right or to the left from the word that he has spoken to thee.*

Neither limb nor muscle has moved or stirred at this, nor is there in my heart any thought or evil counsel concerning this.

But I am of joyful and cheerful heart in this matter, and I say, Blessed is the Lord who has this day chosen me to be a burnt offering before Him. (v.52-56, emphasis added)

Together they built the altar through tears. Then Isaac showed the depth of his humility and resolve with his request of his father.

And Isaac said to his father, *Bind me securely and then place me upon the altar lest I should turn and move, and break loose from the force of the knife upon my flesh and thereof profane the burnt offering; and Abraham did so.* (v. 61, emphasis added)

Then Isaac asked his father to look after Sarah, his mother . . .

And Abraham heard the words of Isaac, and he lifted up his voice and wept when Isaac spake these words; and Abraham's tears gushed down upon Isaac his son, and Isaac wept bitterly, and he said to his father, Hasten thou, O my father, and do with me the will of the Lord our God as He has commanded thee (v.63).

The spirit of total submission is shown in the battle between their hearts and their eyes.

And *the hearts of Abraham and Isaac rejoiced at this thing which the Lord had commanded them; but the eye wept bitterly whilst the heart rejoiced.*

And Abraham bound his son Isaac, and placed him on the altar upon the wood, and Isaac stretched forth his neck upon the altar before his father, and Abraham stretched forth his hand to take the knife to slay his son as a burnt offering before the Lord. . . .

At that time the Lord appeared unto Abraham, and called to him, from heaven, and said unto him, *Lay not thine hand upon the lad, neither do thou any thing unto him, for now I know that thou fearest God in performing this act, and in not withholding thy son, thine only son, from me.*

And Abraham lifted up his eyes and saw, and behold, *a ram was caught in a thicket* by his horns; that was the ram which the Lord God had created in the earth in the day that he made earth and heaven.

For the Lord had prepared this ram from that day, to be a burnt offering instead of Isaac. (v.64-65, 69-71, emphasis added)

THE CALL TO CONSECRATION IN MARRIAGE

Marriage provides glorious opportunities to practice consecration. Just as Isaac was willing to give his life as the ultimate expression of commitment to God, so we are invited to dedicate our lives, our talents, our weekends, and our weaknesses to the sacred enterprise of sanctifying our marriages and ultimately perfecting our souls.

In the day-to-day struggles of marriage we may fail to see that this ultimate sacrifice qualifies us for the ultimate reward. We shall "inherit thrones, kingdoms, principalities, and powers, dominions, all heights and depths"—all that the Father hath (see D&C 132:19)!

This total willingness to sacrifice must not be misunderstood. This is not the same as becoming a gelatinous blob with no form or purpose. This ultimate sacrifice is combined with obedience and informed by the gospel of Jesus Christ to provide an appropriate sacrifice. As God would have it, our whole-soul offerings are likely to bless our partners even as they refine us.

Most of our sacrifices take a startlingly pedestrian form. I have never yet been called on to stand in traffic at risk of life and limb in order to protect Nancy. But I have been called on to make a thousand sacrifices that felt earth-shaking.

For example, I like to squeeze the toothpaste very systematically from the bottom of the tube making sure that every particle is methodically herded toward the nozzle and filling the measure of its creation. After emptying any part of the tube, I fold it so that none of the toothpaste can retreat and hide. I can easily justify my system as tidy and frugal. When Nancy grabs the tube in the middle and thoughtlessly squeezes, a shudder runs through my soul. She seems like a good person . . . how could she act in such a reckless way?

Just as a Book of Mormon king was willing to give away all his sins to know God (Alma 22:18), I must be willing to give away all my petty preferences in order to know the godliness in Nancy's soul. I don't lecture her or condescend to her. I may explain my method, but when it is clear that she is not going to be a conscientious paste-herder, I simply buy a clip to clamp on my tidy folds.

Of course this applies to toothpaste, dirty socks, and messy kitchen counters—and much more! Maybe nothing in the universe would hurt us more than knowing that our partners had flirted with another person. Perhaps the deepest pain we could experience in mortality was finding that our partners had been unfaithful. Perhaps name-calling and insults would injure us seemingly beyond repair. Maybe having a partner who no longer seems to appreciate us might wound us so deeply that we would think the relationship is doomed.

At that critical juncture—and all others—consecration invites us to put everything we have on the altar—to hold nothing back. We are willing to minister to a mixed-up spouse. We are willing to love a failing partner. We bless those who belittle us. We pray for those who have despitefully used us. Please note that no partner should have to tolerate physical violence. In such cases, counseling should be sought. But every married person must accept abundant limitations if they hope to have a strong relationship. Then consecration moves us from acceptance to using our spiritual energy to rescue our imperfect partners.

Consecration has everything to do with marriage. It is much more than "staying together for the kids." It is acting to redeem our partners and our covenants with everything we have and everything we may draw from Heaven. We do all of this in order to establish Zion in our homes.

It took decades for me to realize the significance of the covenant I made with God and Nancy. On that January day more than 30 years ago, I promised God that I would always look for the good in Nancy. I promised that my attitude would always be redemptive—that no sac-rifice would be too great. I promised God that I would be His partner in protecting, blessing, comforting, and saving Nancy's precious soul. After all, there is nothing in God's work I will ever do that will be more important than blessing my covenant partner.

I wish I had realized all that I was promising as part of my covenants on that blessed day. Maybe I would have been a better—a more consecrated—partner all along the way.

Following Christ's example

Recently a good man wrote to me with a great insight: "I have realized that much of my unhappiness in marriage is due to my expectation of love to be shown in a certain way and my withholding love when not feeling loved myself. I have also realized that although I rarely overtly expressed myself, my thoughts and feelings towards my wife have some-times been overly judgmental and critical."

This kind and earnest man demonstrates yet again that the natural spouse is an enemy to marriage. We enter marriage expecting our needs to be met. We even decide how they should be met. Then, when our partners are unable to meet all of our needs, we become resentful. Our distance and resentment are communicated in subtle—or direct—ways. But the message is clear: "You are not a very good spouse. You are a dis-appointment. Until you make some major changes, I cannot really love and appreciate you."

It is common for discontented partners to lament, "I just can't tol-erate the loneliness [conflict, pain, etc.] in this marriage. I must get out in order to thrive."

I think that is how Jesus felt in the Garden of Gethsemane. "Is there any way out? I don't think I can bear it!" Yet He did bear it. And in bearing it, He saved us. Had He not honored His covenant over His peace and comfort, all of us would be everlastingly lost.

The same is true in mortal marriage. No partner on the face of the earth can meet all our needs. In mortality, we will live with disappoint-ment. We can dwell on our discontent or we can celebrate the points of connection. Brother Kent Brooks of the BYU faculty of Church History and Doctrine observed: "Our capacity to love a spouse deeply and our ability to experience great joy in marriage are commensurate with the degree to which we are willing to suffer and hurt, to labor and toil, and to persevere through moments of unhappiness, stress, disappointment, and tests of our patience and love for our partners."[67]

And here is another irony. Those who will bear whatever is necessary in order to honor their covenants will be made glorious. They will experience eternal joy. They are, after all, those who have honored eternal things above temporal things.

This truth is portrayed powerfully in James Farrell's book, *The Peacegiver.* Brother Farrell shows that most of our discontents are caused by our shriveled, narrow views of our partners. When we have the mind of Christ, there is no one we cannot fully love nor gladly serve. [I recommend the book or CD to all!].[68]

We can follow Christ's example and act to serve and redeem our partners, or we can crab and complain that we have not gotten what we deserve.

GIVING GLADLY AND WHOLEHEARTEDLY

There is a popular trend toward encouraging equity in marriage. The emphasis is on sharing household duties in fair ways. There is a lot of merit in having men contribute more to the many household tasks that make a house run smoothly. In most cases women are badly overloaded and men are under-involved at home. Remedying the imbalance is worthy.

The problem with equity is in the inevitable scorekeeping that accompanies efforts toward it. Seeking equity encourages people to think about and value their own contributions. At the same time, humans almost always under-notice and under-appreciate the efforts of others. Anything that encourages this natural-man tendency is destructive.

There is a better way. We can gladly offer our best efforts. We appreciate all that our partners offer. When we have unmet needs, we humbly invite: "I could sure use a hand with putting the kids to bed tonight. Is this something you could help me with?" We give gladly and we receive graciously. Hugh Nibley made this point well: "So the gifts of God are to be received in the same unstinting and joyful spirit in which they are given—freely, magnanimously, *never counting the cost.*"[69]

Rather than carefully tracking every investment in our marriage, we give gladly and wholeheartedly. We give everything we have and are. And we ask God to increase our capacity so we can give yet more.

John Gottman's research on marriage shows that partners who exchange equal numbers of positives and negatives are not those who are happily married. Though it may sound like a 50-50 relationship, they are at high risk of divorce. In contrast, the best indicator that a relationship would be loving and enduring was five positives for each negative! Rather than act as a careful investor, happy marriage partners throw open the doors of the storehouse and give kindness, help, and goodness.

OUR WHOLE SOULS AS AN OFFERING

Brigham Young described the way some of the saints lived the law of consecration. Each of us might consider if our offerings in marriage are of the same broken-down quality as the pioneer offerings he described.

> Some were disposed to do right with their surplus property, and once in a while you would find a man who had a cow which he considered surplus, but generally she was of the class that would kick a person's hat off, or eyes out, or the wolves had eaten off her teats. You would once in a while find a man who had a horse that he considered surplus, but at the same time he had the ringbone, was broken-winded, spavined in both legs, had the pole evil at one end of the neck and a fistula at the other, and both knees sprung.[70]

Do we bring our greatest generosity and richest forgiving to our marriages? Do we offer our whole souls and our best efforts as an offering (see Omni 1:26)? Or do our partnerships get half-hearted, occasional efforts? Our marriages are ideal places to practice the law of consecration.

THE CONSECRATION IN COMMITMENT

Consecration has dimensions of both depth and length. We offer our whole souls—depth. We also continue to serve and love patiently over time—length. God has always asked us to endure to the end.

While some may argue that they do not care to be sealed eternally to the spiritual pygmies who are their partners, those who understand the things of God know that their imperfect partners will one day be made glorious. One day we may feel honored to have known the people we now disdain.

Even science shows the blessing of persistence. Research found that 86 percent of those who reported being unhappy in their marriages, but who did not divorce, five years later described their marriage as either "very happy" or "quite happy."[71]

THE BLESSINGS OF CONSECRATION

I suspect that God designed consecration to move us from peevish, self-serving humanness to sweet, redemptive godliness. I remember when I was the junior companion to my grandfather on our assigned home teaching route. Grandpa Percy had been a prominent man in the community and the Church. He had served as bishop or stake president for over 30 years. But, by the time we were home teaching companions, I thought of him as merely an old man.

I remember home teaching visits to the Ramseyer family. It seemed to my 16-year-old soul that Grandpa told the same tired old stories every time we went visiting—predictable and uninteresting to my teen sensibilities. My mind wandered off to things of greater interest to me.

Grandpa died the summer after I graduated from high school. Now, decades later, I yearn to know more about Grandpa's life. I have collected his papers and photos, and I have studied them. I cannot say how much I would pay to hear those "tired old stories" just one more time. I yearn to hear the jokes, the inflection, the laughter, the tenderness. I would love to record them, transcribe them, memorize them.

But they are gone.

Appreciating the "everyday" in marriage

This is much like mundane marriage. It may seem tedious and trivial. Our minds—and our hearts—may wander. But those who consecrate themselves to their marriage by bringing their whole souls as an offering to the everyday events of a relationship are building a storehouse of sweet memories. They are building an eternal relationship one brick at a time.

The Lord is speaking to each of us when He says:

Verily, verily, I say unto you, ye are little children, and ye have not as yet understood how great blessings the Father hath in his own hands and prepared for you;

And ye cannot bear all things now; nevertheless, be of good cheer, for I will lead you along. The kingdom is yours and the blessings thereof are yours, and the riches of eternity are yours. *And he who receiveth all things with thankfulness shall be made glorious;* and the things of this earth shall be added unto him, even an hundred fold, yea, more (D&C 78: 17-19, emphasis added).

Consecration is a covenant that moves us from asking how we can get our needs met to asking how we can bless and serve. We become more grateful. Rather than wondering if this marriage is a good investment that will pay us a handsome return, we ask for heavenly grace that we may love and serve as Jesus served—without thought of reward. While there are destructive relationships that should end, the vast majority of relationships can survive and flourish if each of us brings our whole soul as an offering (see Omni 1:26).

As Michael Novak observed, dedication to marriage not only blesses our partners but enlarges our souls.

Marriage is an assault upon the lonely, atomic ego. Marriage is a threat to the solitary individual. Marriage does impose grueling, humbling, baffling, and frustrating responsibilities. Yet, marriage is not the enemy of moral development in adults. Quite the opposite. Being married and having children has impressed on my mind certain lessons, for whose learning I cannot help being grateful. My bonds to [my family] are, I know, my liberation. They force me to be a different sort of human being, in a way in which I want and need to be forced.[72]

Consecration in marriage is not simply about receiving our entrance card to the Celestial Kingdom. It's also about becoming *qualified* for the life we will presumably be living there. This requires a transformation of character. In serving and giving to those within our family stewardship as well as demonstrating patience and continually forgiving our spouses for all the ways they might not meet our expectations, we have the opportunity to emulate Christ, thus transforming ourselves.

We witness one of the many gospel ironies. Those who relentlessly demand something better—more attentive partners and better family life—will be disappointed. Those who give up everything—their time, talents, and expectations in service of their families—are the ones who get everything— Eternal Life and Glory.

When we see our challenges within marriage as customized invitations to greater goodness, we will rejoice in His perfect purposes. When we understand our marriages to be the best opportunity we will ever have to show our generosity of spirit, we will be ready to be the kind of partners God would have us be. When we recognize consecration as the training that prepares us for Heaven, we will finally know that *consecration is a blessing.*

CREATING YOUR OWN STORY

Thoughts

Are you willing to exercise full-fledged faith in God—faith that He led you to this relationship and will bless and refine you in it? Will you, with Isaac, "do all that the Lord spoke to thee with joy and cheerfulness of heart"?

Before we married most of us expected marriage to be much like the Garden of Eden. Having been cast out of that unreasonable expectation, what sacrifices are you willing to bring to the altar of your relationship?

Feelings

In the early years of marriage, most of us are bothered by little habits and eccentricities in our partners. These things may not be wrong or bad, they are just different from our experience and preference. They can become a major irritation. As we become more spiritually mature, we are more likely to enjoy our partner as a total package. Have you set aside minor complaints and given your whole heart to your spouse? What can you do to make a more complete offering?

Actions

Are you willing to try a 30-day experiment? For 30 days are you willing to show nothing but kindness and appreciation to your partner? Are you willing to set aside complaints and disappointments and see the good intentions and best efforts in your partner? Rather than count the cost, will you consider seeing the investment as Paul did? He said, "I consider everything a loss compared to the surpassing greatness of knowing Christ Jesus my Lord, for whose sake I have lost all things. I consider them rubbish, that I may gain Christ" (NIV, Philippians 3:8). Are you willing to invest your whole soul in the hope that you will gain eternal joy?

NOTES
_____

64 Ezra Taft Benson, *The Teachings of Ezra Taft Benson,* Salt Lake City: Bookcraft [1988], 121.

65 Neal A. Maxwell, *The Neal A. Maxwell Quote Book,* Salt Lake City: Bookcraft [1997], 62.

66 *Lectures on Faith,* 58, emphasis added.

67 Douglas E. Brinley and D. K. Judd (Eds.), *Living in a Covenant Marriage,* Salt Lake City: Deseret Book [2004], 104.

68 See James L. Farrell, *The Peacegiver: How Christ Offers to Heal our Hearts and Homes,* Salt Lake City: Deseret Book [2004].

69 *Collected Works of Hugh Nibley,* 9:46, emphasis added.

70 *Journal of Discourses,* 2:307.

71 *Covenant Marriage,* 104.

72 *Harper's Magazine,* April 1976, page 37.

Chapter Seven

Charity:

"Pray unto the Father with all the energy of heart,
that ye may be filled with this love."

We are commanded to seek charity "with all the energy of heart" (Moroni 7:48). We are told that we are nothing without it. "Wherefore, my beloved brethren, if ye have not charity, ye are nothing, for charity never faileth. Wherefore, cleave unto charity, which is the greatest of all, for all things must fail—But *charity is the pure love of Christ,* and it endureth forever" (Moroni 7:46-47).

Yet charity may be one of the rarest of gems in this mortal world. Exactly what is it? What does it look like in our lives? How do we get it? And what difference does it make in marriage?

What is charity?

In an effort to understand charity, it is important to know what it is NOT. It is not artificial good cheer. It is not a thin veneer of politeness on a distressed soul. It is not holding our tongues while judging and resenting others. Rather it is a sacred and heavenly gift: "But charity is the pure love of Christ, and it endureth forever; and whoso is found possessed of it at the last day, it shall be well with him" (Moroni 7:47, emphasis added).

Humans do not find charity coming easily or automatically. C.S.

Lewis said:

> When I come to my evening prayers and try to reckon up the sins of
> the day, nine times out of ten the most obvious one is some sin
> against charity; I have sulked or snapped or sneered or snubbed or
> stormed. And the excuse that immediately springs to my mind is that
> the provocation was so sudden and unexpected: I was caught off my
> guard. . . . [Yet] surely what a man does when he is taken off his
> guard is the best evidence for what sort of a man he is. Surely what
> pops out before the man has time to put on a disguise is the truth. If
> there are rats in the cellar you are most likely to see them if you go in
> very suddenly. But the suddenness does not create the rats: it only
> prevents them from hiding. In the same way the suddenness of the
> provocation does not make me an ill-tempered man: it only shows
> me what an ill-tempered man I am. The rats are always there in the
> cellar but if you go in shouting and noisily they will have taken cover
> before you switch on the light. Apparently the rats of resentment and
> vindictiveness are always there in the cellar of my soul.[73]

The natural man is likely to find that resentment and vindictive-
ness come more easily than charity. More than we realize, those negative reactions are a choice—a choice to see in a human, judgmental
way. But we can also choose to see in a heavenly and loving way. That
choice makes all the difference. Charity can be the lens through which
we see each other.

As in all things, Jesus is the perfect example of charity. He is also
our unfailing mentor as we work to develop charity.

A contrast in charity

Jesus was invited to dine with Simon the Pharisee (Luke 7:36-50). It
would be interesting to know Simon's motivation for inviting Jesus over
for a meal. Apparently Jesus was the talk of the town. It seems to me
that Simon's attitude was much like that of David Lettermen when he
has a distasteful guest on his talk show. It is possible to be curious with-

out being cordial.

On a collision course with the dinner party was a woman who was known to be a sinner. We don't know the details of her sin. Was she a tramp and a prostitute? Had she been a blight on the community conscience for years? Was she shunned in the marketplace and streets?

And why was she seeking Jesus? Had she heard Him speak and felt the first stirrings of hope in her soul? Had she seen how He treated those who were injured and imperfect? Had He caught her eye in the street and she felt the first stirrings of pure love she had ever felt?

As Simon's group reclined at the meal in the little courtyard in his home, the unnamed woman burst in. Bad enough that she was a woman and uninvited; adding insult to injury, she was a flagrant sinner! And she touched Jesus, a rabbi! That alone was an offence against Jewish law. She certainly was maudlin; she wept profusely, letting her tears flood His feet. She even anointed His feet with oil no doubt gained through unholy means.

Simon cringed at the mere presence of the woman. And the fact that Jesus tolerated her was a sure sign of His spiritual failings. He had neither discernment nor good manners.

Jesus recognized Simon's small-mindedness. Jesus had the power to humiliate Simon for his shriveled hard-heartedness. He didn't. Instead, he invited him to another way of seeing and being. He asked Simon whether a debtor that had been forgiven a large debt would be more or less grateful than one forgiven a small debt.

Simon shrugged. "I suppose the one forgiven the larger debt."

Then Jesus invited Simon to see what He saw. In a sense Jesus said, in effect, "Simon, you have treated me with coldness and disdain from the moment I set foot in your house. You have not shown even the fundamental courtesies. In contrast, this woman who has no social obligations to me has poured out every devotion and kindness. Her many sins are forgiven because she loved abundantly. Meanwhile those to whom little is forgiven, seem to love little."

Then Jesus turned fully to the woman and spoke cherished words: "Thy sins are forgiven" (Luke 7:48). Picture the radiance of hope emanating from that tear-stained face!

Simon and his crew still did not get the message. In their cold hearts they muttered, "Who does he think he, is presuming to forgive sins?"

WE ARE PLAYERS IN THE DRAMA

In some ways, this is an ideal story for marriage. Think of the woman as the spouse coming to us burdened with sins but wanting something better.

We then have a choice. We can be like Simon and say, "I want nothing to do with a filthy tramp like you. I want and deserve someone better." We can be judgmental and condescending.

Or we can be like Jesus, seeing beyond the burden of sin to a soul struggling to be better. We can, with Jesus, say, "I forgive you of mistakes, shortcomings, and humanness. I welcome you into the fellowship of my love."

In each interaction we choose to be a Simon or a saint. We choose to see each other the way ordinary mortals see each other, or we choose to see each other the way Jesus sees us. That is charity, the mind of Christ.

Marvin J. Aston explains this principle well: "Perhaps the greatest charity comes when we are kind to each other, when we don't judge or categorize someone else, when we simply give each other the benefit of the doubt or remain quiet. Charity is accepting someone's differences, weaknesses, and shortcomings; having patience with someone who has let us down."[74]

There are many other ways this amazing story can be applied to our lives. Every one of us is a beggar at the throne of heavenly grace. Every one of us needs forgiveness for sins. So we come to Him as the woman came to Him. We fall at His feet and weep with humble recognition of our failings. We anoint His feet with everything precious we have. We know we do not deserve the kindness He shows and the forgiveness He grants. But we are grateful for every encouragement. We are all dependent upon His charity.

THINKING ABOUT CHARITY

Elder Max Caldwell of the Seventy gave useful insights on charity.[75] (I am presenting the principles in a different order than he did.) He observes that the common use of the word charity is different from its doctrinal or scriptural use. "The phrase 'love of Christ' might have meaning in three dimensions: Love for Christ, Love *from* Christ, and Love *like* Christ."

Charity is first and foremost the redemptive love that Jesus offers all of us. It is the love from Christ. He is the model of charity—which never faileth. As Elder Maxwell observes, "His relentless redemptiveness exceeds [our] recurring wrongs."[76] Or, in the words of the hymn, Jesus implores us:

At the throne I intercede; For thee ever do I plead.
I have loved thee as thy friend, With a love that cannot end.
Be obedient, I implore, Prayerful, watchful, evermore,
And be constant unto me, That thy Savior I may be.[77]

He did all He did so He can save us. "For God sent not his Son into the world to condemn the world; but that the world through him might be saved" (John 3:17).

If you are like me, you may have resisted God's love most of your life. I believed with all my heart that God loved all His children—while resisting His love for me personally. After all, not only did I sin, but I sinned knowingly and deliberately. How could He possibly love me?

Yet He reaches after us. Somewhere along the path, the miracle of His love breaks down our resistance. As we begin to understand His goodness and redemptiveness, we are changed. We are filled with a profound awe and gratitude for Him. We experience the stirrings of hope. Without this conversion, we are nothing spiritually (1 Corinthians. 13:2; 2 Nephi. 26:30; Moroni 7: 44, 46; D&C 18:19).

As the amazing truth of His unrelenting love pierces our hearts, we are led to the second kind of charity, love *for* Christ. "We love *him,* because he *first loved us*" (1 John 1:19, emphasis added). I am not sure if these first two dimensions of charity can be disentangled. As soon as we glimpse His love for us, we instinctively love Him in return. We fall at His feet and bathe them with tears of gratitude. Why would He do all He has done to love and rescue my flawed soul? Why???

THE ANSWER IS: CHARITY.

As we feel the love from Him and for Him, we naturally love like Him. We become saviors on Mount Zion with Him. "This love which thou hast had for the children of men is charity" (Ether 12:34). The surest mark of discipleship is a love for all people—i.e., charity.

The scriptures are clear that this third kind of charity is inextricably tied to a love for God.

"If a man say, I *love* God, and hateth his brother, he is a liar: for he that loveth not his brother whom he hath seen, how can he *love* God whom he hath not seen?" (1 John 4:20, emphasis added).

He who washed the disciples' feet and wore Himself out in serving them and rescuing them gave us this astounding command: "A new commandment I give unto you, That ye love one another; *as I have loved you*" (John 13:34; emphasis added).

We are to become partners with Him in the great work of salvation. We are to be swallowed up in love from Him, for Him, and like Him. Elder Caldwell concluded, "charity sustains us in every need and influences us in every decision."

WHAT DOES CHARITY LOOK LIKE IN REAL LIFE?

Let's first consider what it does NOT look like. How does the natural man see others? Let's return to an online question that I first quoted in the introduction:

After thirteen years of marriage, I've come to realize that I really don't like my wife. She is everything that I despise in a wife and a person. I'm a Christian man and have tried everything the books say, have taken direct orders from our pastor to implement actions all in an effort to cause a positive change in the marriage. The bottom line is, I see no positive aspects to my wife's personality and it taints all of her relationships, especially ours. I really dislike being around her and I've run out of solutions. Just short of divorce, is there anything that can be done as a final effort to salvage this marriage? B.C. in NM.

Ouch! "She is everything that I despise!" The online response was sensible:

There were probably several things you enjoyed about your wife when you married her. After a while, differences become irritants for most of us who are married. Then we make a critical choice. Will the irritants be the basis for blaming or for compassion? When we react with blame, it usually worsens the condition we hate. We see more faults and feel more irritated. In our own ways we all contribute to our own unhappiness.

There is an alternative. At every critical juncture we can choose compassion. We can choose understanding, patience, and personal growth. We can, as Gottman suggests, "find the glory in our marital story." We can use our differences to balance each other and to spur growth.

It is my view that most of us have misunderstood the purpose of marriage. It is not a picnic with friends. It is more like a college education with occasional joys, lots of growth, and abundant homework.

There may be too much pain in your marriage to rescue your relationship, but if you can see her and your marriage objectives differently, there might be hope for a close and satisfying relationship.

We are all familiar with the lack of charity. We have all felt the critical, negative, carping, nit-picking, fault-finding, and grousing attitude that comes easily to the natural man. Charity does not flow automatically from having an extraordinary spouse. It is primarily the result of the way we choose to see each other.

AN EXAMPLE OF CHARITY

Instead of inconveniences and irritations, some see goodness and blessings. One of my heroes is John Glenn. He is a hero because of his pioneering space accomplishments, both as a young man and as a mature man. He was a conscientious politician. But perhaps he was most heroic in his marriage.

John and Annie grew up together. They played together as children and dated through high school. John described Annie as "pretty, with dark hair and a shy, bright smile." They were in band, glee club and YMCA/YWCA together.

However, there were challenges. Some classmates teased Annie for her severe stuttering, but John didn't see her stuttering as a problem. "It was just something she did, no different from some people writing left-handed and others right-handed. I thought it was cruel and thoughtless to laugh at someone for something like that—especially Annie, whom I cared for—and I told them so."[78]

Annie's stuttering made it almost impossible for her to shop alone. She would have to write a description of what she wanted and show it to a clerk because she was not able to ask for it. Any public appearance was painful for Annie. Yet John lived a very public life.

At one point when John was preparing for a space launch, he got a message to call Annie. Vice President Johnson wanted to visit their home. Annie refused. John was threatened that his place in the space program could be in jeopardy.

Most of us might have fared poorly as husbands in such a situation. We might have called our wives and said "Look, I'm risking my life for the country; can't you simply step out of your comfort zone and meet with the vice president?" In our hearts we might have accused, "Why must you think only of yourself." We tolerate imperfections in our partners until they inconvenience us. Then we expect change.

But John Glenn was different. "Annie wouldn't have refused to see the vice president without a really good reason . . . I told her whatever she wanted to do, I would back her 100 percent."[79]

Years later John Glenn was considered as a running mate for Jimmy

Carter. Reportedly, he was not chosen in part because of Annie's stutter. "It shocked us and it hurt."[80] However, once out of the political race, John Glenn joked that he was free to mow the lawn at home.

At one point, Annie took an intensive course to help her overcome stuttering. After the three weeks of grueling training, John described her homecoming:

> "John," she said when she got home, hiding an impish smile, "I've wanted to tell you this for years: Pick up your socks." . . . Annie grasped the gift of speech and held it tight. Our lives were transformed. Our phone bill increased as she started calling friends around the country.[81]

John Glenn might have been irritated many times by Annie's stuttering, her quietness, and the impact they had on his life and career. But he wasn't. He helped her. He saw past her impediment.

John Glenn's accomplishments as a pilot and an astronaut are remarkable. His strength of character is commendable. Yet his greatest accomplishment may have been the kindness and tenderness he showed his wife, Annie. Though he might have been irritated many times by Annie's stuttering, her reticence, and the impact they had on his life and career, he never showed that. Instead he loved his Annie.

OUR OWN HEARTS STUTTER

In some ways Annie's stuttering is a great symbol for the large tracts of territory in our character where the natural man still rules. Each of us has weaknesses, "thorns in the flesh." When we see weaknesses in our partners, it is easy to be annoyed. In fact our own weaknesses—which *should* make us humble—may make us even more annoyed by our partners' weaknesses.

We will continue to be annoyed by our spouses unless we are humbled enough by our own limitations to call on heavenly grace. Paul called on heaven for relief from his limitations. When the relief did not come, he set the example for all of us with his attitude:

And he said unto me, *My grace is sufficient for thee:* for my strength is made perfect in *weakness.* Most gladly therefore will I rather glory in my infirmities, that the power of Christ may rest upon me.

Therefore I take pleasure in infirmities, in reproaches, in necessities, in persecutions, in distresses for Christ's sake: *for when I am weak, then am I strong.* (2 Corinthians 12: 9-10, emphasis added)

This is one of many gospel ironies. It is only when we recognize our weakness that we can be made strong by His perfect grace.

How do we get charity?

How do we obtain the precious gift of charity? Note carefully:

Wherefore, my beloved brethren, pray unto the Father *with all the energy of heart, that ye may be filled with this love,* which he hath bestowed upon all who are *true followers of his Son, Jesus Christ;* that ye may become the sons of God; that when he shall appear we shall be like him, for we shall see him as he is; that we may have this hope; that we may be purified even as he is pure. Amen (Moroni 7:47-8, emphasis added).

The answer is clear. We receive charity as we become true followers of Jesus Christ and we beseech Him for the gift. We must want it with all our hearts.

Putting charity into perspective

I have tried to make sense of the two great triads in scripture. The first principles and ordinances of the gospel are faith, repentance and covenants (which includes both baptism and confirmation). The scriptures also talk about faith, hope, and charity. How do the two triads relate to each other?

I have wondered if the former are the commandments that guide our choices and the latter are the fruits of our choices. Perhaps faith as a desire to believe results in faith as an inner assurance. Perhaps repentance—turning our sins over to Jesus—leads to hope—that sense that Jesus can and will save us. Perhaps entering into covenants of baptism, the sacrament, and any personal covenants we make with God direct us to charity, the mind of Christ.

God's command- ments, our choices	Faith—putting the desire to believe into action	Repentance— giving our sins to Him and acknowledging our weakness	Covenants— baptism,sacrament, and personal covenants
Fruits of our choices	Faith—the inner assurance of God's reality and goodness	Hope that Christ's Atonement can reach to *me* and those I love	Charity—taking on the character of Christ

Charity is the culminating gift of our spiritual seeking. "And now abideth faith, hope, charity, these three; but the greatest of these is charity" (1 Corinthians 13:13).

Charity comes only when we humbly recognize the weakness of our mortal natures and throw ourselves on the *merits,* and *mercy,* and *grace* of the Holy Messiah (2 Nephi 2:8, emphasis added). The Book of Mormon teaches clearly and repeatedly that "there shall be no other name given nor any other way nor *means* whereby salvation can come unto the children of men, only in and through the name of Christ, the Lord Omnipotent" (Mosiah 3:1, emphasis added 7).

WHAT DIFFERENCE DOES CHARITY MAKE IN MARRIAGE?

It seems that every relationship faces an Abrahamic test. Somewhere along the way some challenge surfaces that seems insurmountable. It may be a spouse with a temper, one who will not be close and affectionate, or pornography and unfaithfulness. These challenges are insurmountable—unless we have charity. We simply will not survive and thrive in the challenges of marriage unless we take upon ourselves the mindset that Jesus has. His redemptive mindset is called charity. (This is not to suggest that we should merely shrug at major violations of trust. Appropriate action is needed. Yet, whatever else is appropriate, charity is still essential.)

It is important to note that charity is necessary not only for big challenges but also for the small chafings of daily life. All who have been married more than an hour have felt irritated with their spouses. Some people, like my dear wife, hardly let irritations rise to the level of awareness. She almost always shrugs them off.

I do a much better job of representing the fallen human race. I chafe about word choice in a simple statement she makes. I grumble about indecision. I grouse that she doesn't know that I don't like celery—let alone celery soup. I moan when she is late (even though I am late far more often than she), and I gripe when the table is set with the knives facing the wrong direction. My unchanged soul protests such violations of order and propriety.

I have repented a lot in almost four decades of marriage. I am learning little by little to see as the Lord sees. I am learning to follow President Joseph F. Smith's counsel:

> We all have our weaknesses and failings. Sometimes the husband sees a failing in his wife, and he upbraids her with it. Sometimes the wife feels that her husband has not done just the right thing, and she upbraids him. What good does it do? Is not forgiveness better? Is not charity better? Is not love better? Isn't it better not to speak of faults, not to magnify weaknesses by iterating and reiterating them? Isn't that better? And will not the union that has been cemented between you and the birth of children and by the bond of the new and everlasting covenant, be more secure when you forget to mention weaknesses and faults one of another? Is it not better to drop them and say nothing about them—bury them and *speak only of the good that you know and feel, one for another, and thus bury each other's faults and not magnify them; isn't that better?*[82]

A similar thought has been expressed by a wise observer: "How delightful is the company of generous people, who overlook trifles and keep their minds instinctively fixed on whatever is good and positive in the world about them. People of small caliber are always carping. They are bent on showing their own superiority, their knowledge or prowess or good breeding. But magnanimous people have no vanity, they have no jealousy, and they feed on the true and the solid wherever they find it. And, what is more, they find it everywhere."[83]

We can test the power of charity by reflecting on those who have shown us charity. It softens us. It causes us to relax. It brings out the best in us. Even those of such strong character and great spirituality as the Prophet Joseph Smith have experienced the power of kindness. "Nothing is so much calculated to lead people to forsake sin as to take them by the hand, and watch over them with tenderness. When persons manifest the least kindness and love to me, O what power it has over my mind, while the opposite course has a tendency to harrow up all the harsh feelings and depress the human mind."[84]

When we choose to see the good, think about it, talk about it, and appreciate it, we bless those around us—often by evoking the same attitude in them. This can cascade us to Zion.

KEEPING OUR FOCUS

At some point in your marriage, like me, you have probably enjoyed at least 80% of your spouse's traits. Even then, there is that bedeviling 20% that still annoys us. Most of our marriage-fixing efforts are focused on that bothersome 20% of our partner's character that we just can't find a way to enjoy.

We notice, study, analyze, and organize our lists of our partners' faults. Then we either undertake a deliberate spousal improvement project or—in weak moments—we explode with complaint. Anyone who has objectively observed human nature knows the effect of either cool or hot criticism: it creates discouragement and defensiveness.

The failure of our partners to appreciate our analyses of their characters is likely to result in more analysis and more criticism. Over time the marginal discontent can become the focus of our relationship. What a tragedy.

Such tampering with spousal character, though well-intended, is simply not effective. Criticism does not lead to repentance and growth; It leads to anger, defensiveness, and distance.

The human preference for support was well expressed by Noel Coward: "I love criticism just so long as it's unqualified praise." In other words, most of us would prefer that our partners think about the 80% of us they like rather than dabble with the 20% they don't like.

As Wendy Watson observed, "the best-kept secret in many marriages is the strengths spouses see in each other. . . . An interesting fact about commending your spouse is that the more you do it, the more you see in him or her to commend."[85]

SOME THINGS NEVER CHANGE!

John Gottman has made interesting discoveries about that 20% that we don't like. He has discovered that approximately 70% of what we don't like will never change! We can be mad about that. We can feel cheated. But heaven seems to have constructed that percentage and it is not likely to change!

What a wise design! Rather than re-working our partners to our liking, we are invited to cover their weaknesses with our charity! God is serious about cultivating our charity. Irritations with our partners are not a challenge to diplomacy as much as to our charity. There are no right words when our hearts are wrong.

Of course we can divorce the disappointing spouse and marry someone different—someone who doesn't irritate us in the way our spouse does. And we may be happy . . . for a time. However, every relationship comes with irresolvable differences. That seems to be a law of nature.

On average, it takes two years for couples to realize that their marital differences will stubbornly remain a part of their relationship. After that "honeymoon" with one spouse, we can divorce, marry someone new, and enjoy a new honeymoon—for a short time. Inevitably we will find a new set of problems with the new partner. Rather than hitchhiking down the marital road, God invites us to stop, make a commitment, and cultivate our aptitude for appreciation.

Those of you who are careful accountants may be thinking that if 70% can't change, what about the remaining 30% of what we don't like that *can* change. There is another intriguing irony here. According to Gottman's thorough research, the ONLY way to get partners to change that 30% is by enjoying them the way they are! You can spot the irony. When we love our partners the way they are, we don't care if they change! That is the very thing that liberates them to change. Acceptance is the key to change in those areas where it is possible.

So the messages of research and the gospel are the same: We should enjoy and appreciate our partners. We should forgive them of their humanness. The single most promising marriage-fixing effort is not tinkering with our partners' characters; it is in loving, cherishing, and appreciating them!

This fits with the research discovery that partners in happy marriages see qualities in their spouses that even the spouses' best friends don't see! Good marriage partners become serious talent scouts. In fact, like good parents who exaggerate their children's good qualities, good marriage partners are likely to exaggerate their spouses' strengths.

BETTER WAYS: TOOLS FOR CHARITABLE LIVING

There are several keys to charity. They are no surprise. We must be humble enough to recognize our own failings. We must have faith unto repentance, that is, we must trust Jesus enough to be willing to run to Him with our sins, begging for His help with managing our mortal selves and changing our natures.

Consider the case of the woman who was rushing from one evening duty to the next. As she passed her husband, she sighed, "I'm so tired."

An unwise husband might give unwelcome advice: "Why don't you lie down for a minute?" A wiser husband knows that his wife's words have special meaning even if he doesn't know what the meaning is. Kent R. Brooks teaches us how to discover those special meanings: "We need to let our partners teach us how to meet their underlying needs. . . . Save for the influence of the divine, the best authority we have on how to meet the needs of our spouse is our spouse!"

He may not know the meaning. But he is open to being taught. So he might say things such as:

"Today has been a burdensome day?" "You sound worn out." "Tell me more about what you're feeling."

As his wife describes the special meaning of her words to him, he gets better ideas for how he can help. Maybe he is tired too. If so, he may call on Heavenly resources, "Father, give me the strength and the goodness to help my dear wife."

He might also call out for pizza. The best response to her statement depends on the special meanings it has for her. Marleen S. Williams underscores the central role of seeing through the eyes of our partners: "When you understand another person through the lens of his or her own life experience and history, you will find it easier to interpret that person's behavior accurately and to learn how to accommodate differences."[87]

THE FORMULA FOR SPIRITUAL POWER

In the great section of the Doctrine and Covenants in which the Prophet Joseph Smith cried out for relief for the Saints and vengeance on enemies, the Lord taught Joseph the principles of heavenly power. Near the conclusion of the section, God gave the formula. Notice the two keys:

> Let thy bowels also be full of *charity towards all men,* and [especially those in your own home], and *let virtue garnish thy thoughts unceasingly;* then shall thy confidence wax strong in the presence of God; and the doctrine of the priesthood shall distil upon thy soul as the dews from heaven.

> The Holy Ghost shall be thy constant companion, and thy scepter

an unchanging scepter of righteousness and truth; and thy dominion shall be an everlasting dominion, and without compulsory
means it shall flow unto thee forever and ever. (D&C 121:45-46,
emphasis and paraphrase added)

It appears that charity and virtue are the keys to accessing heaven's
power. Consider a couple of examples. Terry Olson shares an excellent
example of lubricating life with charity. He describes a situation where
many of us would be annoyed and abrasive. Yet this man apparently
had (at least on this occasion) risen above the natural-man reaction.

> The wife of a long-distance truck driver is worried about dinner
> being late. She and her husband always celebrate his return from his
> three or four days on the road with a quiet dinner. Although he is a
> little later than she expected, she is grateful she has not yet heard the
> brakes of the big rig in front of the house, because she wants the
> whole thing to be ready, and it's not. Alas, there is the noise she had
> been both dreading and hoping for. She begins to imagine his com-
> ing in the back door, hanging up his jacket and then, before washing
> up, leaning around the hall entrance and smiling a greeting. She wor-
> ries he will see the unset table and discover the unready meal. She is
> worried that his face will fall, that he will think his homecoming is
> no longer a big deal or will not include the spirit of welcome she typ-
> ically offers. In other words, she is imagining him being offended—
> perhaps even resentful—at her unpreparedness. She worries he will
> hold it against her. Her imaginings seem absolutely realistic to her.
>
> Her husband, however, presents her with an alternative reality. When
> he actually does lean around the corner and sees that dinner prepa-
> rations are incomplete, he smiles, catches her eye, and says, "Hi,
> honey. Looks like I got here just in time to help. Be right there."[88]

In an honest story of transformation, an anonymous author tells in
the *Ensign* of moving from frustration and judgment to appreciation and
love—to charity.[89] She and her husband fought regularly. She got to the
point where she neither loved nor liked him. She felt trapped. She could

have miserable singleness or miserable marriage. She prayed. A new thought came to mind. She could stay, love her husband, and be happy.

Unfortunately, her best efforts to conjure up some love for her husband were fruitless. She did nice things for him—but he didn't notice. After three weeks of sincere effort, nothing was better. She begged God to change her husband. God invited her to change herself. Having already given her best effort, she didn't know what else to do, but continued to pray for help. In Gospel Doctrine class the answer came as they read Mormon's invitation to pray with all the energy of heart for charity.

She began trying to see her husband as Jesus saw him. And she felt invited to look for the good in him. At first this was very hard. Although she found it much more natural to catalogue his faults, she started looking for his positive qualities.

The author reports that something wonderful was happening within her. She began to realize that her husband wasn't the big jerk she had thought him to be. He had many wonderful traits that had been overlooked or forgotten. Then came a second blessing. In the absence of nagging, her husband started dropping many of the bad habits she had pestered him about.

Though their relationship had improved, she still felt no love for her husband. She prayed more earnestly. She reports that one day she looked across the table at him, and suddenly, was filled with an intense love for him. Tears filled her eyes. She suddenly saw him as her eternal companion, whom she loved more than words could express. She felt his infinite worth and wondered how she had ever overlooked it. She sensed the Savior's love for him.

That is the blessing we all seek. It is the heavenly gift that changes everything.

CREATING YOUR OWN STORY

Thoughts

Look for good qualities and kind deeds by your partner. Don't discount their goodness by looking for imperfect motives. Notice the good.

Appreciate it.

Reflect on the wisdom of sages:

"Fill us with Thyself, that we may no longer be a burden to ourselves."[90]

"How much larger your life would be if [you] could become smaller in it. . . . You would begin to be interested in [others]. You would break out of this tiny . . . theatre in which your own little plot is always being played, and you would find yourself under a freer sky, in a street full of splendid strangers."[91]

Feelings

Pray with all the energy of heart for charity. Make it the desire of your heart.

Actions

According to the scriptures, we love Him because He first loved us (1 John 4:19). The same can apply to marriage. Our partners will love us because we first love them. Love first. Don't wait to be loved.

NOTES
_____

73   C.S. Lewis, *Mere Christianity*, New York: Macmillan [1960], 164-65.

74   "The Tongue Can Be a Sharp Sword," *Ensign*, May 1992, 19.

75   "Love of Christ," *Ensign*, Nov. 1992, 29.

76   "Jesus of Nazareth, Savior and King," *Ensign*, May 1976, 26.

77   "Reverently and Meekly Now," *Hymns*, no. 185, verse 4.

78   John Glenn and Nick Taylor, *John Glenn: A Memoir*, New York: Bantam Books, [1999],3

79   *Memoir*, 252-53.

80   *Memoir*, 335.

81   *Memoir*, 325-327.

82   *Teachings of the Presidents of the Church: Joseph F. Smith*, Salt Lake City: The Church of Jesus Christ of Latter-day Saints [1998], 180-81, emphasis added.

83   Van Wyck Brooks, *A Chillmark Miscellany*.

84 *Teachings of the Prophet Joseph Smith,* 240.

85 "Love and Marriage," *BYU Magazine* [Spring 2002], page 59.

86 *Covenant Marriage,* 97.

87 *Covenant Marriage,* 77.

88 *Covenant Marriage,* 125.

89 See Name Withheld, "Falling Out of Love and Climbing Back In," *Ensign,* Jan. 2005,50.

90 Harry Emerson Fosdick, *The Meaning of Faith,* New York: Association Press [1918], 213

91 Gilbert K. Chesterton, *Orthodoxy,* [1959], 20-12.

HEAVENLY MARRIAGE:

"Have ye experienced this mighty change in your hearts?"

THE NATURAL MAN'S WAY IN MARRIAGE

There is one little ploy that is at the center of most of the world's work on marriage. It is called active listening. It involves re-stating what your partner has said until he or she is fully satisfied that you understand. Only then can you express yourself. After you have had your say, your partner must re-state *your* feelings until you are satisfied.

Most prominent marriage programs and untold numbers of marriage books have active listening as their centerpiece. Marriage training drills the skill endlessly in the hope that it can become second nature and rescue marriage from a slide into rancor and divorce.

If you take potato salad that has been left out in the hot summer weather for a full week and trying to reclaim it by putting a fresh layer of egg slices and a sprig of parsley on top, the salad is still rotten. It is almost certain to make you sick. In similar fashion active listening cannot cover up malicious intent. For people who are basically good and earnestly committed to marriage, active listening may help them understand each other. But if the potato salad is permeated with salmonella, no amount of garnish will make it good for you.

A soul is like potato salad. When our souls are permeated with accusation and demands, there is no skill that can cover our malice and meanness.

Terry Warner poses a question that invites us to think in a entirely different way than we usually do. He suggests that the key to happy relationships is not finding gentle-sounding ways to request change. Instead, "what would happen if we dropped all charges against those around us and, for their sakes, happily sacrificed all bitter satisfaction, all retribution, all demand for repayment, all vengeance without regret or second thoughts?"[92]

Catherine Thomas observes that we often get it all backwards: "Much of the emotional pain that we have does not come from the love that we were not given in the past, but from the love we ourselves are not giving in the present."[93]

We need more than a set of skills for expressing discontent and requesting changes. We need a change of heart. The only way to build a truly healthy marriage is by being a truly good person—to be changed in our very natures: "And now behold, I ask of you, my brethren of the church, have ye spiritually been born of God? Have ye received his image in your countenances? Have ye experienced this mighty change in your hearts?" (Alma 5:14).

Unfortunately this is an elusive goal for mortals. We become good in fits and starts. In fact as we conquer one errant habit, a flock of others gets away from us. Self-improvement is an unpromising enterprise.

There is only one way

King Benjamin described the only way to get to goodness: "And moreover, I say unto you, that there shall be no other name given nor any other way nor means whereby salvation can come unto the children of men, only in and through the name of Christ, the Lord Omnipotent" (Mosiah 3:17).

We may have failed to apply to marriage wise words quoted by President Benson: "You do change human nature, your own human nature, if you surrender it to Christ. Human nature can be changed here and now. Human nature has been changed in the past. Human nature must be changed on an enormous scale in the future, unless the world is to be drowned in its own blood. And only Christ can change it."[94]

THE FORMULA FOR CHANGE

Jimmy Townsend has joked that "marriage teaches you loyalty, forbearance, self-restraint, meekness and a great many other things you wouldn't need if you had stayed single." The truth is different. We need those qualities whether married or single, but marriage is God's finishing school for the godly soul. Marriage is ordained to stretch and refine us.

Christ is the great change agent, and His process for change is described by the principles and covenants of the Gospel of Jesus Christ. It is the formula for change, growth, and goodness, the only formula with an ironclad guarantee. I have tried to capture the essence of those principles and covenants in the chapters of *Drawing Heaven into Your Marriage*.

Please study the table and think about God's purposes for marriage. (You probably will see vital principles that I have missed. I hope you will add them.)

It seems that God's objective for marriage is not merely to provide us

Drawing Heaven into Your Marriage	*Actions that can change our hearts and redeem our marriages*
Chapter 1: Marriage is ordained of God. *The big picture of His plan*	Expect challenges. Welcome growth. We can act on several levels: telestial, terrestrial or celestial. God will show us the way back.
Chapter 2: Willing to submit in all things. *The principle of sacrifice*	Our natural ways make us enemies to each other. We need a broken heart and contrite spirit. We must be willing to submit to God for our marriages to survive.
Chapter 3: Lord I believe, help Thou mine unbelief. *Faith in the Lord Jesus Christ*	We must resist evil. We cannot flourish without heavenly help. We can use irritation as an invitation to get heavenly help. God is able to do His work.
Chapter 4: O Jesus Thou Son of God, have mercy on me. *Humility and repentance*	We are to fix ourselves and love others, not vice versa. When we focus on discontents, we enlarge them. When we love and accept our partners, they grow. Our pride is conquered by calling out for mercy.

Drawing Heaven into Your Marriage	Actions that can change our hearts and redeem our marriages
Chapter 5: How then can I do this great wickedness and sin against God? *Purity in marriage*	Satan uses mischief and deception to turn our hearts from our partners. He is subtle. When we choose purity, we are blessed and enriched. There is no way to have a great relationship without focusing our love on our spouses.
Chapter 6: Zion cannot be built up unless it is by the principles of the celestial kingdom. *Consecration in marriage*	We must be willing to put everything on the altar. Each may be asked to make some Abrahamic sacrifice. Every day we must make tiny sacrifices of convenience or preference.
Chapter 7: Pray unto the Father with all the energy of heart, that ye may be filled with this love. *Charity in a healthy marriage*	When we see our partners as Christ does, we love them. His grace is sufficient to turn our weakness into strength. Love is a choice including the choice to see and celebrate the good in our partners.

companionship through the treacherous journey of mortality—though it often does that wonderfully well. Marriage is not merely for populating the world—though it can accomplish that.

God has loftier purposes. He wants to make us like Him. Phew! Like Him! "Unto the measure of the stature of the fullness of Christ" (Ephesians 4:13)!

Resisting God

If you are like me, you resist the possibility on the personal level: He may be able to turn Brother or Sister So-and-so into beings like Him—but I am far too weak and imperfect.

One particular experience challenged my resistance. When I was serving as a bishop, a new member of the ward approached me after sacrament meeting and asked for an interview. We made an appointment for that afternoon. At the appointed time she came. We prayed together.

Then she launched into the tragedy of her life. She told of abuse and immorality and ugliness and betrayal that stretched from her child-hood to her current life. I sat with a peaceful facade but inner horror and disbelief. I had never heard such a tale of awfulness. What could I tell her? How could her life ever be straightened out? What hope could she ever have of healthy relationships and a productive life? She had never been more than a marginal Mormon and she had no apparent resources. It almost seemed that suicide was her only hope.

The dreaded moment came. "Bishop, what can I do?" I was amazed to hear myself saying, "There are three things the Lord would have you do." I had no idea what those three things were.

I took a blank piece of paper from the desk drawer and said, "Number 1 is . . ." and the Lord dictated the first item of hopeful and specific counsel. In like manner the Lord dictated the second and third items. We discussed them and sent her on her way with a hope she had never before known.

After she left the office, I closed the door behind her and fell to my knees. "Lord, I didn't know. I just didn't know how much you love your children. I had no idea you could make something fine out of the mass of confusion that is our lives. I didn't know."

That is His greatest miracle. He can make us divine. I no longer remember the three items of instruction that He gave to that burdened woman that day. But I could no longer resist Him. I realized that, if the Lord loved that woman with her terrible life, He also loved me with all my failings. So I simply submitted to His love. I could not compre-hend why He would love me—but I knew that He did. I accepted it without understanding it.

You, dear reader, may be wiser than I was. You may have already accepted that life-changing love. If so, you know that He works with us line-upon-line shaping us into something holy. If you have not yet accepted that love, I beg you to open your heart to it. Accepting His love makes all the difference.

A NEW PATH TO SALVATION

We cannot save ourselves. Only He can save us. He wants to save us.

Stephen Robinson summarized our situation in his book, *Following Christ:*

> So the great divide between the saved and the unsaved, between those who inherit the kingdom and those who do not, between those who are right with God and those who are not, isn't just who is "good" and who is "bad," for technically speaking we are all bad in some degree. Rather, the great divide is whether we accept or reject the covenant with the Savior Jesus Christ, the only being in eternity who can make us innocent by incorporating us into his infinite, perfect, and sinless self.[95]

A related message is taught in the story of the prodigal son. Elder Bruce D. Porter reminds us that "the parable of the prodigal son is a parable of us all. It reminds us that we are, in some measure, prodigal sons and daughters of our Father in Heaven. For, as the Apostle Paul wrote, 'all have sinned, and come short of the glory of God'" (Rom. 3:23).[96] Sister Henrie's poetic rendering of the great story reminds us of the One who waits for each of us at the gate.

To Any Who Have Watched for a Son's Returning
By Mary Lyman Henrie

He watched his son gather all the goods
that were his lot,
anxious to be gone from tending flocks,
the dullness of the fields.
He stood by the olive tree gate long
after the caravan disappeared
where the road climbs the hills
on the far side of the valley,
into infinity.
Through changing seasons he spent the light
in a great chair, facing the far country,
and that speck of road on the horizon.

Mocking friends: "He will not come."
Whispering servants: "The old man
has lost his senses."
A chiding son: "You should not have let him go."
A grieving wife: "You need rest and sleep."
She covered his drooping shoulders,
his callused knees, when east winds blew chill, until that day
A form familiar, even at infinity,
in shreds, alone, stumbling over pebbles.
"When he was a great way off,
His father saw him,
and had compassion, and ran,
and fell on his neck, and kissed him.[97]

We can flee Him or we can go to Him. It is always better to go to Him. When we choose to follow Christ, we choose to be changed, as President Benson reminded us.

HE IS OUR ADVOCATE

Jesus has given us good reason to trust Him. For example, He tells us in some detail what to expect at the judgment bar.

We half expect Him to lead the way into heaven. Before He heads to His 40 acres by Kolob Lake, He wishes us well: "I hope you make it. I know you tried. Maybe it will be okay." Then He is gone.

As we wait in line, we wonder if there will be a scripture chase. Will we have to know all the books of the Old Testament in order? Will there be a spreadsheet of all the months we didn't get our home or visiting teaching done? Will we have to account for each of our sins, weaknesses and omissions? Will others in line laugh as the failure-ridden video of my life is shown? Worst of all, will He be standing across the table from me shaking His head in disappointment as all my life's thoughts and actions are reviewed?

That is what we expect. But that is not what He does. He does not leave us facing Father alone. In Doctrine and Covenants section 45, He tells us why we should listen to Him.

Listen to him who is the advocate with the Father, who is pleading
your cause before him— (v.3).

One very good reason to listen to Him is because He is our advocate with the Father. He is the One who will present us to Father. He
is pleading our cause. He is the only One who can get us in. We must
trust Him.

In the scriptural account He tells us just how He will present us:
"Saying: Father, behold the sufferings and death of him who did no sin,
in whom thou wast well pleased; behold the blood of thy Son which
was shed, the blood of him whom thou gavest that thyself might be
glorified" (D&C 45:4).

We might wonder why He is saying so much about His amazing
life and infinite sacrifice. It makes our own stained life seem all the
more awful. How will this help us? Sure, He will be glorified, but what's
to be done with me? How can I ever enter where the Gods dwell?

Jesus continues: "Wherefore, Father, spare these my brethren that
believe on my name, that they may come unto me and have everlasting
life" (D&C 45:5).

A thunderbolt! A total surprise! He presented the merits of His life
and goodness in order to win my way into Heaven! He did what He
did in order to save my soul!

One by one He pushes every believer into Heaven before He
Himself makes His final entrance. We who are last are pushed in first
while He who is First in all things enters behind the last saint. Whether
we are timid or tortured, He will find and recover every last stray sheep
before He Himself enters. What a shepherd he is!

The biggest surprise in all of God's creation is that "His relentless
redemptiveness exceeds my recurring wrongs," as Elder Maxwell testi-
fied. Or, as Janice Tindall magnificently wrote:

Burning with Light
   My soul quivers
   At thy touch.
Oh God, my God

God of my fathers
Wonderful, Counsellor,
Prince of Peace.
There is no mountain high enough
Nor ocean deep enough
Nor desert wide enough
To glorify thy name.[98]

A PARTNER IN THE PROCESS

I know that I can never be anything without Him. I am grateful that He is willing to labor to refine and rescue my flawed soul.

There are others to whom I owe a debt of gratitude. I am grateful for children who strive to live noble lives. I am grateful to noble parents who taught me so much about God and goodness. I am thankful to ancestors who continue to sustain us.

Yet there is one person I thank above all but Jesus. Her name is Nancy. I wish I could be objective about Nancy, but I cannot. She is mild in temperament—we laugh in the family that she is by constitution and disposition unable to yell.

She is very compassionate—she seems naturally drawn to those who are lonely or disenfranchised. She is unselfish—she demands no gifts or considerations. Yet she is glad to serve—it will take half of eternity for me to repay all the backrubs she has given me in 30-plus years of marriage.

She has a gentle and clever sense of humor—only those who listen carefully get to enjoy it.

She is devoted—her children and grandchildren know that her love is stronger than the cords of death for she would gladly die for any one of them—and they know it.

She is uncomplaining—I was first drawn to her when, on a single adult activity, she fell in a bitter cold river and climbed into the raft laughing. In addition, she is beautiful—I love her sweet face and lovely frame.

As if that were not enough, she is also the kindest person I have ever known–bar none.

I regularly thank Heavenly Father for blessing me with a companion who is far better than I knew and far finer than I deserve. I cannot imagine life without Nancy.

So, why is it that I sometimes get irritated, impatient or judgmental of my dear companion? How can I explain patches of discontent?

After decades of episodic analyzing and blaming, I have discovered that my feelings about Nancy are not as much a measure of her as of me. Just as our feelings about God are a good measure of our faith, so our feelings about our companions are a reliable gauge to our personal goodness.

So why do we mortals build our dramas of discontent? How do we transform our early love into simmering (or seething) discontent?

Learning the lessons

I should note that I do not believe that every marriage can make it. But the great mass of quiet-desperation marriages do not need divorce but need only more charity in order to flourish. The Gospel of Jesus Christ is the cure for the common marital complaint.

Jesus is not only the Creator of worlds but the Energizer of relationships. In Him all things have life. As He said: "The thief [Satan and his servants] cometh not, but for to steal, and to kill, and to destroy: I am come that they might have life, and that they might have it more abundantly" (John 10:10).

Abundantly indeed. If I am unhappy with Nancy it is because I do not understand or do not honor the covenants I have made. I do not have charity. I believe that the covenant of consecration together with the marriage covenants effectively require me to promise God: "I now covenant with Thee that from this time forth and forever I will never see any fault in Nancy." It is not enough just to stay in the marriage in solemn determination while occasionally mowing the lawn. I believe that God expects me to consecrate not only my time but also my thoughts! Even my feelings!

Certainly it is better to light a candle on our partners' qualities than to curse the darkness that can be found in every soul. When I am unhappy with Nancy in any way, it means that I need to get a spiritual tune-up. As in the Lord's great parable, having been forgiven a fifteen billion dollar debt, how can I fail to forgive Nancy her fifteen dollar (or fifteen cent) debts?

I think God designed marriage to help us grow spiritually. The most important lessons I have learned about being a good person I did not learn on my mission, sitting in High Priest quorum, or serving as bishop; I learned them in marriage. But it has taken three decades of work to go from a selfish clod who complains, to a marginal-saint who adores his companion. I thank Heavenly Father for the priceless lessons He has taught me about the sweet joy of love.

AN INVITATION

I end this exploration of marriage with Moroni's concluding invitation and a few editorial additions of my own:

> Yea, come unto Christ, and be perfected in him,
> [Only He can make us perfect!]
>
> and deny yourselves of all ungodliness;
> [especially the complaining and criticizing that is abundant in mortality]
> and if ye shall deny yourselves of all ungodliness,
> and love God with all your might, mind and strength,
> then is his grace sufficient for you,
> that by his grace ye may be perfect in Christ;
> [Perfect in Christ! He will carry us with His merits while we struggle to be better. What good news!]
> and if by the grace of God ye are perfect in Christ, ye can in nowise deny the power of God.
> [His greatest miracle is the work He does to redeem our souls!] (Moroni 10:32).

He can make us perfect. I invite all readers to join me as we fill ourselves with the doctrine of Christ and make covenants with the Giver of Life. By this process we become the people and partners God invites us to be. As our remarkable Redeemer makes us at-one with God, He also makes us at-one with our partners. What a blessing! What a gift!

May God bless our marriages. Or, as in President Benson's great benedictory on us: "May we be convinced that Jesus is the Christ, choose to follow Him, be changed for Him, captained by Him, consumed in Him, and born again I pray in the name of Jesus Christ, amen."[99]

CREATING YOUR OWN STORY

Thoughts

Read over the following prayer which was quoted earlier in this book. Enjoy the prayer's sense of trusting submission. Consider whether it is a prayer you would like to take to Father:

> Lord, I know not what I ought to ask of thee; Thou only knowest what I need; Thou lovest me better than I know how to love myself. O Father! give to Thy child that which he himself knows not how to ask. I dare not ask either for crosses or consolations: I simply present myself before Thee, I open my heart to Thee. . . . Smite, or heal; depress me, or raise me up: I adore all thy purposes without knowing them; I am silent; I offer myself in sacrifice; I yield myself to Thee; I would have no other desire than to accomplish Thy will. Teach me to pray. Pray Thyself in me. Amen.[100]

Feelings

Alma asks us a searching question: "can you imagine to yourselves that ye hear the voice of the Lord, saying unto you, in that day: Come unto me ye blessed, for behold, your works have been the works of righteousness upon the face of the earth? . . . I say unto you, can ye look up to God at that day with a pure heart and clean hands? I say unto you, can you look up, having the image of God engraven upon your countenances? (Alma 5:16, 19). How would it feel if we imagine the same things for ourselves? Maybe the thought will motivate us to come faithfully and humbly to the sacrament table begging the Savior to haul off our accumulated sins. The sacred rendezvous with Jesus at the sacrament table is our only hope for arriving Home clean and right. Alma continues his lesson: "I say unto you, ye will know at that day that ye cannot be saved; for there can no man be saved except his garments are washed white; yea, his garments must be purified until they are cleansed from all stain, through the blood of him of whom it has been spoken by our fathers, who should come to redeem his people from their sins" (Alma 5:21).

Actions

As we are filled with the Gospel of Jesus Christ, we are inclined to act redemptively. We are less inclined to be irritated and more inclined to be helpful. In what ways can you help your spouse along the journey toward Heaven?

NOTES

92 Quoted by Catherine Thomas, *Zion and the Spirit of At-one-ment*, Provo, UT: FARMS

93 *Zion,* 5.

94 Ezra Taft Benson, "Born of God," *Ensign,* Nov. 1985, 5-6.

95 Stephen E. Robinson, *Following Christ,* Salt Lake City: Deseret Book [1995], 6, emphasis added.

96 "Redeemer of Israel," *Ensign,* Nov. 1995, 15.

97 *Ensign,* March 1983, 63.

98 "Triptych," *Ensign,* July 1992, 49.

99 Ezra Taft Benson, "Born of God," *Ensign,* November 1985, 6

100 Francois de la Mothe Fenelon quoted in Harry Emerson Fosdick, *Meaning of Prayer,* 58-59.

EPILOGUE

Fairly often someone calls me at home or at work and tells me their marriage is in trouble. They ask if they can come see me. I explain that I am a professor of family life but not a therapist. That almost never deters them.

They—usually a couple but sometimes one partner—set an appointment to come to see me. They are always in deep pain (which motivates them to come). I often do something they don't expect. They come prepared to process a litany of complaints and a load of discouragement. They often expect me to be able to sort it out and equip them with a new tool for relationship repair.

That is not what I do. Instead I ask them to tell me about a time when things have been great in their marriage—when they have felt close, loving, and happy. Being able to do that is a very good sign which means they have not destroyed the possibility of love.

A MORE EXCELLENT WAY

As they speak of good times, I am amazed at the distinct and remarkable talents that are manifest. For example, it may become clear that one has great compassion and the other has a delightful sense of humor. In another couple one may be a careful, practical thinker and the other exuberant. Whatever the combination, their strengths are almost immediately evident.

And so is the trouble. Our strengths unfailingly get us in trouble. Not only do we overuse them so that they become a major irritation to our spouses, but they also under-gird the fundamental falsehood of marriage: we think we can make things right. We assume that we can work through our differences if we just use our God-given talents.

WE ARE MISTAKEN

We cannot create a vibrant marriage out of two people regardless of their talents, penchants, or country of origin. It is not possible. We must have divine help. "Nevertheless neither is the man without the woman, neither the woman without the man, in the Lord" (I Corinthians 11:11).

The Lord must be a partner if a relationship is to prosper. In fact He must be the ruling partner. There is no other way to have a vibrant relationship.

While there are those who have never heard His name who have healthy relationships, I believe that they must operate by His principles if they are to have a strong relationship. The Light of Christ lights every man and woman who comes to mortality. That Light knows that He is the Way, the Truth, and the Life. No man or woman comes to a healthy relationship without His prospering principles.

His formula for growth and well-being—and for a happy marriage—is very different from that described by the world. In fact it is counter to that prescribed by the world. I return to a familiar and challenging passage: "And if men come unto me I will show unto them their weakness. I give unto men weakness that they may be humble; and my grace is sufficient for all men that humble themselves before me; for if they humble themselves before me, and have faith in me, then will I make weak things become strong unto them" (Ether 12:27).

Notice the key elements. Our weakness is divinely appointed. It is intentional and heaven-sent. And it has one purpose: to make us humble.

That is a big surprise. God gave us weakness so we would recognize our dependence on Him. Our central task is to make ourselves (with the help of our weakness) humble. Then, as we turn our lives over to Him, He will make us clean and holy.

TESTING THE FORMULA

Here is a way to test this formula. Think of times when you have been completely at peace with God—when you have felt His goodness and love. How did that feeling of rightness with Heaven affect your marriage? I'm guessing that you could tolerate any amount of disappointment and misunderstanding as long as you felt close to God. It is the magic potion, the heavenly elixir.

So the enemy desperately wants to prevent that. He wants to get us thinking not about God's goodness but about our partner's failings. He wants us to be filled with them. He knows that rumination and recrimination put us in his filthy hands.

Satan knows that healing human souls is something we humans always do poorly. That is why the devil wants us to be mate-fixing do-it-yourselfers.

This is a keen irony in our dilemma. We cannot fix our partners. We cannot even fix ourselves! But we can make ourselves humble. We can recognize our dependence on God for all that we have and are. We can gladly acknowledge that it is He who lends us breath and sustains the simplest functions of life and love.

So when we presume to set our partners and our marriage right, we are intruding on the Heavenly prerogative. We are seizing the reins from God. It doesn't work. We mortals make poor gods.

What does work is to recognize our weakness and beseech God for that divine gift of charity. Rather than tamper with our partner's soul, we can throw ourselves on the merits, mercy and grace of Him who is mighty to save. Only when filled with heavenly light can we offer heal-ing love to our partner.

This is fully foreign to the natural man—that same natural man who is an enemy to God. We want to fix our marriages using our own insights and wisdom. But, when we recognize that we never see the big picture, that we cannot look into our partner's soul, and that there is only One who sees perfectly, then we are on the path to healthy partnership.

A MIGHTY CHANGE

It is miraculous to me to describe these truths to the couples who come to see me and watch them become peaceful as they lean into His able arms. We are not responsible to fix the universe—or even our mar-riages. We are to cheerfully do all that we are able to do. Then we ask God to make up the difference—which is vast for all humans.

My testimony is that the puny mortal who leans on God is far more powerful than any humanist armed with any measure of talent and training. King Benjamin challenges us to recognize that we do not know all things that God knows (see Mosiah 4:9). We are not able and God is.

As I testify of these truths, those couples who are most spiritually mature weep with joy. They soften as they turn themselves and their lives to the One by whom we are made sons and daughters unto God. They have faith unto repentance—that is, they trust God enough to turn themselves over to Him. This is President Benson's powerful mes-sage from his Christmas devotional:

> Men and women who turn their lives over to God will discover that He can make a lot more out of their lives than they can. He will deepen their joys, expand their vision, quicken their minds, strengthen their muscles, lift their spirits, multiply their blessings, increase their opportunities, comfort their souls, raise up friends, and pour out peace. Whoever will lose his life in the service of God will find eternal life.[101]

THE STRUGGLE

Because the formula is simple does not mean that it is easy. Most of us guard our independence quite jealously. Even when we are convinced that we should turn ourselves over to God, the natural man fights and kicks against the effort.

Yet the disciples who repent, regularly and gladly, find a growing goodness in their lives. They find God taking up occupancy in their souls. They are changed.

In my experience, it does not take 25 sessions of therapy to work through our marital woes; It does take thousands of occasions when we turn our souls over to God. The Holy Ghost delivers the shiver of recognition not only in sacred places but even as we ride in the car mulling over our irritations. He invites us to kindly helpfulness even as we arrive home tempted to deliver a corrective sermon. He points us toward compassion even as we are tempted to condescend toward the ones to whom we are joined by covenant.

All eternity hangs in the balance. Will we respond to the invitation? I pray that we will—again and again—until He calls us forth and presents us to Father as those who trusted in Him. On that holy day our knees will humbly bow and our tongues gladly confess that Jesus is the Christ—the one who saves our souls, changes our hearts, and rescues our relationships.

NOTES _____

101   Ezra Taft Benson, *Teachings of Ezra Taft Benson,* Salt Lake City, UT: Bookcraft [1988], 361.

RECOMMENDED READING

HIGHEST RECOMMENDATION:

All scripture. God knows and teaches the process for having our natures changed.

AMONG THE BEST (IN DESCENDING ORDER OF IMPORTANCE):

Robinson, Stephen E. *Believing Christ*. 1993. [As we are filled with the doctrine of the atonement, we are more likely to be gracious in marriage. This book is a must-read!]

Gottman, John M. *The Seven Principles for Making Marriage Work*.1999. [One of the most solid books on marriage, this teaches core principles from extensive research.]

Farrell, James L. *The Peacegiver*. 2004. [Brother Farrell helps us see how our self-deception gets in the way of our marriages.]

Christensen, Andrew and Neil Jacobsen. *Reconcilable Differences*. 2000. [Acceptance is a vital part of good marriage.]

Love, Pat and Steven Stosny. *How to Improve Your Marriage without Talking about It*. 2007. [Men want respect, women want closeness. The ways we act deliver the opposite.]

Gottman, John. *Why Marriages Succeed or Fail*. 1994. [Discusses three kinds of relationships and the blessings and challenges of each.]

Gottman, John M. *The Relationship Cure*. 2001. [Especially good section on bids, i.e., our efforts to connect, and the ways we can respond to bids.]

Gottman, John M. and Julie Schwartz Gottman. *10 Lessons to Transform Your Marriage*. 2006. [Ten case studies to help each of us see how to apply the principles that strengthen marriages.]

Goddard, H. Wallace and James P. Marshall. *The Marriage Garden,* 2007 at www.arfamilies.org. [Six lessons on key principles of marriage.]

VERY GOOD BOOKS (IN ALPHABETICAL ORDER BY AUTHOR'S LAST NAME):

Arbinger Institute. *Leadership and Self-Deception: Getting Out of the Box.* 2000. [Self-deception exacts a terrible cost at work and at home.]

Beck, Aaron T. *Love is Never Enough*. 1988. [Strong marriages require more than a strong feeling. Ideas for changing the way you think about problems.]

Doherty, William J. *Take Back Your Marriage*. 2001. [Don't let the world pull you apart.]

Fowers, Blaine J. *Beyond the Myth of Marital Happiness*. 2000. [Insightful book about the importance of values in sustaining marriage.]

Glass, Shirley P. and Jean Coppock Staeheli. *Not "Just Friends:" Protect Your Relationship from Infidelity and Heal the Trauma of Betrayal*. 2003. [Affairs can be prevented or overcome.]

Stanley, Scott. *The Heart of Commitment.* 1998. [Commitment is a key to a strong relationship.]

Waite, Linda & Maggie Gallagher. *The Case for Marriage*. 2000. [Describes the many benefits of marriage.]

Weiner-Davis, Michelle. *The Divorce Remedy*. 2001. [How to prevent divorce.]

Weiner-Davis, Michelle. *The Sex-Starved Marriage*. 2003. [Physical intimacy is a challenge for many couples.]

ABOUT THE AUTHOR

H. Wallace Goddard, Ph. D., is a Professor and Family Life Specialist with the University of Arkansas Cooperative Extension Service. He has created numerous family programs and a PBS television series. His previous books include *The Soft-Spoken Parent, The Frightful and Joyous Journey of Family Life, and My Heart Delighteth in the Scriptures: Personal and Family Applications* as well as a revision of the classic *Between Parent and Child.*

Wally has written for *Meridian Magazine* since 1999—the first year it was introduced online. His acquaintance with Scot and Maurine Proctor who publish the magazine was one of those "chance" meetings that was meant to be. He ended up sitting by Maurine at the World Family Policy Forum and they began talking. The subject of *Meridian Magazine* came up and Wally told her about his passion for writing—about some of the very subjects Meridian most wanted to cover. Because of that one serendipitous meeting Wally became one of Meridian's most prolific, most insightful, and most loved columnists.

Wally has served in the Church as a bishop, institute teacher, and high councilor. He and his wife Nancy have three adult children and a growing number of amazing grandchildren. Over the years they have cared for twenty foster children.